Brian Galvin
Chris Kane

Reading Comprehension

VERITAS PREP

Authors	Brian Galvin
	Chris Kane
Co-founders	Markus Moberg
	Chad Troutwine
Contributing Writers	David Newland
	Ashley Newman-Owens
Contributing Editor	Jodi Brandon
Cover Design	Nick Mason
Interior Design	Tom Ahn
	Dennis Anderson

This book is dedicated to Veritas Prep's instructors, whose enthusiasm and experience have contributed mightily to our educational philosophy and our students' success.

It is also dedicated to the teachers who inspired Veritas Prep's instructors. The lesson that follows was only made possible by a lifelong love of learning and of undertaking educational challenges; we have teachers around the world to thank for that.

Finally and most importantly, this book is dedicated to our thousands of students, who have taught us more about teaching and learning than they will ever know. And to you, the reader, thank you for adding yourself to that group.

Personal Dedications

Veritas Prep is a community of educators, students, and support staff, and these books would not be possible without our cast of thousands. We thank you all, but would like to specifically acknowledge the following people for their inspiration:

Clay Christensen (Harvard Business School), Tom Cotner (Plymouth-Salem High School), David Cromwell (Yale School of Management), Lenore Goshorn (Allen Elementary School), Henry Grubb (Fort Osage High School), Dana Jinaru (Beat the GMAT), Patricia Kenney (University of Michigan), Steven Levitt (University of Chicago), Walter Lewin (Massachusetts Institute of Technology), Lawrence Rudner (Graduate Management Admission Council), Jeff Stanzler (University of Michigan), and Robert Weber (Kellogg School of Management).

TABLE OF CONTENTS

CREATING *Think Like the Testmaker*

Creating is the top of the pyramid in Bloom's Taxonomy. When you have completely mastered the GMAT, you are able to Think Like the Testmaker. You are on top of the pyramid looking down! You don't just have good content knowledge and lots of practice with GMAT problems; you understand how a problem has been made, what makes it hard, and how to break it down. When you Think Like the Testmaker you can:

1. Quickly recognize what the problem is actually asking,

2. Discover hidden information and manipulate it to make it useful,

3. Recognize and see through trap answers, and

4. Create your own plan of attack for any problem.

APPLYING *Skills Meet Strategy*

What makes the GMAT difficult is not so much the underlying skills and concepts, but rather the way those skills and concepts are tested. On the GMAT, what you know is only as valuable as what you can do with that knowledge. The Veritas Prep curriculum emphasizes learning through challenging problems so that you can:

1. Learn how to combine skills and strategies to effectively solve any GMAT problem,

2. Most effectively utilize the classroom time you spend with a true GMAT expert, and

3. Stay focused and engaged, even after a long day in the office.

REMEMBERING *Skillbuilder*

In order to test higher-level thinking skills, testmakers must have some underlying content from which to create problems. On the GMAT, this content is primarily:

• Math curriculum through the early high school level, and

• Basic grammar skills through the elementary school level.

To succeed on the GMAT you must have a thorough mastery of this content, but many students already have a relatively strong command of this material. For each content area, we have identified all core skills that simply require refreshing and/or memorizing and have put them in our *Skillbuilder* section. By doing this:

1. Students who need to thoroughly review or relearn these core skills can do so at their own pace, and

2. Students who already have a solid command of the underlying content will not become disengaged because of a tedious review of material they've already mastered.

PREVIEW

As you learned in the Foundations of GMAT Logic lesson, the educational philosophy at Veritas Prep is based on the multi-tiered **Bloom's Taxonomy of Educational Objectives**, which classifies different orders of thinking in terms of understanding and complexity.

To achieve a high score on the GMAT, it is essential that you understand the test from the top of the pyramid. On the pages that follow, you will learn specifically how to achieve that goal and how this lesson in particular relates to the **Veritas Prep Pyramid.**

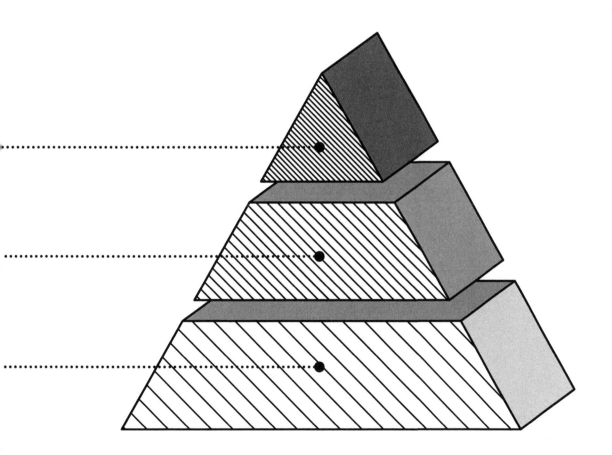

How This Book Is Structured
Our Curriculum Is Designed to Maximize the Value of Your Time

The Veritas Prep Teaching Philosophy: Learning by Doing

Business schools have long featured the Case Method of education, providing students with real-world problems to solve by applying the frameworks they have studied. The Veritas Prep *Learning by Doing* method is similar. In class, you will spend your time applying skills and concepts to challenging GMAT problems, at the same time reviewing and better understanding core skills while focusing your attention on application and strategy. The Case Method in business school maximizes student engagement and develops higher-order thinking skills, because students must apply and create, not just remember. Similarly, the *Learning by Doing* philosophy maximizes the value of your study time, forcing you to engage with difficult questions and develop top-of-the-pyramid reasoning ability.

An important note on *Learning by Doing*: In business school, your goal with a business case is not to simply master the details of a particular company's historical situation, but rather to develop broader understanding of how to apply frameworks to real situations. In this course, you should be certain to reflect on each question not simply through that narrow lens (Did you answer correctly? What key word made the difference?), but rather as an example of larger GMAT strategy (How could the exam bait you with a similar trap? How deeply do you need to understand the content to solve this genre of problem more efficiently?).

As you learned in the Foundations of GMAT Logic lesson, there are important recurring themes that you will see in most GMAT problems:

 THINK LIKE THE TESTMAKER

- Abstraction
- Reverse-Engineering
- Large or Awkward Numbers
- Exploiting Common Mistakes
- Selling the Wrong Answer and Hiding the Correct Answer
- Misdirection
- Content-Specific Themes

 SKILLS MEET STRATEGY

- Guiding Principles
- Problem-Solving Strategies
- Leveraging Assets

REMEMBER: Don't mistake activity for achievement! Focus on recurring themes, not just underlying content.

PREVIEW

Each book in the Veritas Prep curriculum contains four distinct sections:

1. **Skillbuilder.** We strongly suggest that you **complete each Skillbuilder lesson before class** at your own pace, and return to the *Skillbuilder* when you recognize a content deficiency through practice tests and GMAT homework problem sets.

   The *Skillbuilder* section will:

   - Cover content that is **vital to your success on the GMAT**, but is best learned at your own pace outside the classroom.

   - Allow you to **review and/or relearn** the skills, facts, formulas, and content of the GMAT. Each student will have his own set of skills that are "rusty" or even brand-new, and will find other items that come back quickly.

   - **Vary in length** significantly for each book, based on the number of underlying concepts. (For instance, the Advanced Verbal lesson does not have a *Skillbuilder* because you are already building on the concepts introduced in three previous lessons.)

2. **Lesson.** The lessons are designed to provide students with maximum value added from an instructor by:

   - Doing in-class problems together (*Learning by Doing*), and

   - Analyzing those problems for the recurring takeaways.

     With each problem, there will be a detailed explanation that will help you understand how the problem is testing a particular concept or series of concepts, what makes the problem hard, and what underlying skills are required to solve it.

     When relevant, there will be particular boxes for *Think Like the Testmaker*, *Skills Meet Strategy*, and *Skillbuilder* when you should be focused on particular aspects of how the question is made or how the underlying content is being tested.

     NOTE: When doing in-class and homework problems, you should **do your work below the problem,** and you **should *not* circle the answer** on the actual question (just note it on the bottom of the page). That way, if you want to redo problems, you can simply cover up your work and proceed as if you had never done it.

3. **You Oughta Know.** The *You Oughta Know* sections will round out each lesson and cover:

- Obscure topics that arise infrequently.

- More advanced topics that are not common on the GMAT but do get tested.

  While these uncommon content areas do not warrant in-class time, we believe you should have some exposure to these topics before taking the GMAT. Therefore you should **complete these sections before moving to the homework problems**. As with the *Skillbuilders*, the length of these will vary depending on their importance.

4. **Homework Problems.** In many ways, the homework problems are **the most important part of each book.** After refreshing core content in the *Skillbuilder* and then applying that knowledge in the lesson, you must reinforce your understanding with more problems.

   Each question is accompanied by a **detailed explanation** in your online student account, as well as a quick-reference answer key on the last page. A majority of questions are above the 50th percentile in difficulty, and they are arranged in approximate order of difficulty (easiest to most difficult). By completing all of the homework problems, you will learn all of the different iterations of how concepts and skills are tested on the GMAT.

   Homework problems are designed to be challenging, so do not despair if you are answering questions incorrectly as you practice! Your goal should be to learn from every mistake. Students can miss a significant percentage of questions in each book and still score extremely high on the GMAT, provided that they learn from each problem. Embrace the challenge of hard problems and the notion that every mistake you make in practice is one that you will know to avoid on the GMAT when every question counts.

LESSON

Introduction to Reading Comprehension

With reading comprehension, the GMAT is testing an essential skill in business: your ability to scan through dense materials and recognize the significant and relevant information. In business school and beyond, this will be important not only in your daily reading of major newspapers, but also in your ability to sort through tedious business documents and correspondence. Time is at a minimum in the fast-paced business world, and reading efficiently and effectively is arguably the most important skill tested on the GMAT.

At first glance, Reading Comprehension questions might seem like the most familiar of the question types on the GMAT. Everyone has been reading since first grade, and reading comprehension is a part of almost all the major standardized tests. But reading on the GMAT is not pleasure reading; it takes concentration and discipline to focus on the often-convoluted passages about unusual and unfamiliar topics. This exercise is designed to reward those who can efficiently sort through technical jargon and unimportant details to find the relevant takeaways.

To do that effectively, you must adapt your reading strategy to the task at hand. In this lesson, you will learn how to do that with the STOP reading strategy. This essential strategy keeps you from getting bogged down in difficult passages and allows you to save time for the more challenging, detail-oriented questions. These questions typically force you to go back to the passage and carefully analyze a sentence or paragraph. In the third section of the lesson, you will focus on how to contend with these different question types and how to recognize common traps and tricks used by testmakers to make them hard.

On the GMAT, success on Reading Comprehension depends on two major components that will be the focus of this lesson:

- Your ability to read through the passage efficiently, and retain the core information and structure of the passage, and

- Your ability to answer difficult detail-oriented questions that rely on a careful interpretation of specific information in the passage.

Reading Comprehension and the Veritas Prep Pyramid

With Reading Comprehension, the primary underlying skill is something that you have been doing your whole life: reading. But it is important to remember that reading on the GMAT is a unique skill that must be honed for the specific task at hand. Also, you should realize that many of the detail-oriented questions are logically identical to Critical Reasoning questions. The majority of detail-oriented questions are Inference questions and many others ("function" questions in particular) are similar to the "method of reasoning" type that you learned in the Critical Reasoning lesson. Given this, there is no Skillbuilder for the Reading Comp lesson, because the underlying skills are not unique. What is unique is the way you must apply those skills, and that is best taught with the in-class lesson.

In class, you will focus first on the STOP reading strategy, which is the primary focus of the lesson. After that you will learn how to contend with difficult questions and on the "Think Like the Testmaker" thought process. Success on Reading Comprehension questions starts with the middle of the pyramid; you must have the proper reading strategy for the exercise at hand. After you learn to do that well, you must go to the top of the pyramid and understand how testmakers make Reading Comprehension questions difficult. We will cover that in detail in the second half of this lesson and later in the Advanced Verbal book. The following are the core concepts/skills for Reading Comp from the Veritas Prep Pyramid:

 "Core Skills" from Previous Skillbuilders and Lesson:
- Logic
- Critical Reasoning Inference Questions
- Critical Reasoning "Method of Reasoning" Questions

"Skills Meet Strategy" Takeaways from the Lesson Section
- "STOP" Reading Strategy
- Question Specific Strategies
- Leveraging Assets
- Learning by Doing

"Think Like the Testmaker" Takeaways from the Lesson Section
- Selling the Wrong Answer
- Hiding the Correct Answer
- Misdirection
- Abstraction
- Content-Specific Themes

SECTION 1: READING COMPREHENSION BASICS

Your GMAT exam will consist of three or four reading comprehension passages of three to six questions each, accounting for 12 to 14 of your Verbal section questions. The official directions that will appear with each reading comprehension passages are:

The questions in this group are based on the content of a passage. After reading the passage, choose the best answer to each question. Answer all questions following the passage on the basis of what is stated or implied in the passage.

The following rules of the game should serve as a guide while preparing for Reading Comprehension:

1. Each passage comes with three to six questions that appear one at a time to the right of the passage. Since you can only see one question at a time, read the passage first and do not bother previewing the first question; a 90-second to two-minute time investment is appropriate for the initial reading, as you will see several questions based on that passage.

2. Once you have received the passage, the questions that follow are fixed. The Verbal section is adaptive, but not within each passage (you will get the same second question regardless of whether you answered the first correctly or incorrectly).

3. Reading comprehension passages can be up to 350 words. This word limit is new within the last few years. (As recently as 2010, the word limit was as high as 460.) Expect to see dense information in succinct, compact passages.

4. The passage will appear on the left-hand side of your screen the entire time you are working on its associated questions, but the questions to the right will change. You cannot return to questions once you have answered them.

5. The passage may include a vertical scroll bar in the middle of the screen. Be certain to check whether the passage extends beyond the bottom of your screen! Students have in the past reported that they did not recognize this until a few questions into that passage, then realized that their earlier questions were incorrect once they saw the "new" information. Make sure that you have read the entire passage before you begin the questions.

For a look at how the computer screen will look, please consult the diagram below. Note that this diagram comes from an official GMAT Prep practice test, not from a live exam; as such, the screen will look this way but on test day you will not have the option to "check answer."

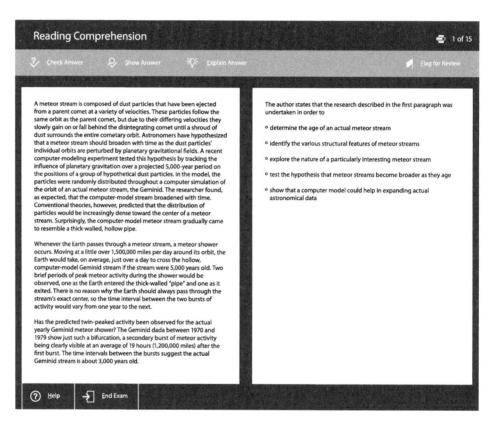

Types of Passages

The GMAT features three broad categories of reading comprehension subject matter:

1. Natural sciences (astronomy, biology, etc.)

2. Social sciences (philosophy, history, etc.)

3. Business-related (business history, economic theory, etc.)

Most test-takers will see at least one of each category, and most test-takers tend to have one genre that they enjoy reading and one that they do not at all enjoy reading. This should not matter! You should read each passage the same way, using the STOP method that you will learn in the following pages. When a topic interests you, you are susceptible to allowing your mind to wander away from what will be important on the questions. When a topic bores or intimidates you, you can still use STOP to set yourself up to answer the questions even if you do not walk away with a deep understanding of the concept. Your mission is simply to answer the questions correctly, so do not let the subject matter throw you off of your plan. The questions themselves are much more important than the passage, much of which simply provides context for the sections that are crucial to the questions.

LESSON

SECTION 2: "STOP" READING STRATEGY

The most important component to success on Reading Comprehension is your reading strategy. The biggest mistake that people make in this exercise is that they read the passage too slowly, getting bogged down in details and trying to understand every detail. The initial reading is only important for answering broader, Universal question types and for retaining overall structure (so you know where to go back for detail-oriented questions). The information that you need to get from your initial reading can be summarized by the acronym STOP:

- **Scope:** From your initial reading you should understand the boundaries of the passage, and specifically how those boundaries relate to the primary purpose.

- **Tone:** From your initial reading you should understand whether there is tone in the passage. This relates specifically to the type of passage, of which there are three on the GMAT:

  o **Explanatory/Descriptive.** The goal of these passages is simply to provide information and/or describe situations or historical events. There will be no purposeful tone in these passages.

  o **Analytical.** The goal of these passages is to analyze some event, theory, and/or information. There is no overt tone, but the passage is not completely objective and will contain some suggestive tone.

  o **Opinionated/Presenting a Hypothesis.** The goal of these is to present an opinion and/or a hypothesis. There will be clear and overt tone in these passages.

- **Organization:** From your initial reading, you should understand broadly the topic of each paragraph and recognize any important transitions in the passage.

- **Purpose:** From your initial reading, you should understand the primary purpose of the passage. Primary purpose relates directly to both scope and tone.

LESSON

Every time that you finish a passage you should complete a mental checklist that covers the following:

1. **What type of passage is this?** This will highlight whether there is tone in the passage and help guide you to the primary purpose.

2. **What is the primary purpose of the passage?** In your own words, you should note why the author has written the passage, carefully considering the boundaries and the type of passage.

3. **What is the topic of each paragraph?** You should have a broad understanding of each paragraph so that you know where to go back for each specific question.

More on Reading Style and Strategy

Now that you understand the basics of STOP, it is important to consider some other important components to reading strategy. **Think of your reading style for these exercises as "speed reading."** With speed reading, the basic approach is to focus only on core information and key summaries and/or transitions. Any section with technical information or specific details should be read quickly, with an eye for summaries or reasons why that information has been given. **Remember: In Reading Comprehension, the information is not nearly as important as why the author has given it to you.** You should pay special attention to important summary and transition words (a detailed list is given in the "Organization" section) and also read carefully at the beginning and end of paragraphs.

Importantly, you must remember that the only goal from this initial reading is to be able to answer Universal, implicit questions (approximately 25% of all questions) and to understand the overall structure of the passage (so you know where to go back for detail-oriented questions). For all detail-oriented questions (approximately 75% of all questions), you must go back to the passage and find the relevant information to answer these questions. Most detail-oriented questions on the GMAT involve information and/or relationships in the passage that you would not consider important in your initial reading. One of the biggest mistakes that people make in reading comprehension is that they read the passage too slowly and then try to answer all questions based on that initial reading. **Reading comprehension is question-driven. You need to get a broad view of the passage in your initial reading and then save most of your time for finding the relevant information to answer detail-oriented questions.**

Before you apply this approach to several passages, consider the following strategies and the reasoning behind them:

- **You should take about 90 seconds on average to read a passage.** Many people will read them in a minute; others (particularly non-native speakers) will need up to two minutes. **You should never take more than two minutes to read a passage.** Remember that the time pressures on the GMAT are extreme, and you want most of your time to contend with tricky, detail-oriented questions for which the initial reading is not very helpful. The longer the passage, the faster you should be reading it, as it will contain more details and unimportant information. The shorter the passage, the slower you should be reading it, as it will be more similar to critical reasoning in which every word matters. If you borrow a little time from Sentence Correction problems (many of which can be answered in 90 seconds), then **you have around eight**

minutes to both read the passage and answer four questions (the average number you get with a passage). As you practice reading comp, set that as your timing goal for a passage with four questions.

- **Honing your reading speed takes lots of practice.** You have to learn how to get the core information that matters, and leave the technical jargon and details behind. If you read too quickly, you will not be able to answer the Universal questions (ones like "what is the primary purpose?"), and if you read too slowly, you will be wasting time that you should use once you have seen the questions. Spend lots of time in your preparation honing this reading style. **Make sure you STOP after each paragraph to mentally note the topic and function of that paragraph.**

- **Don't take notes.** Taking notes is a time-wasting strategy for Reading Comprehension questions that has been pushed by many test prep companies. All you need to have at the end of the passage is a mental note of:

  o Passage type.

  o Primary purpose.

  o Broad subject of each paragraph.

  Importantly, you must remember that you have no idea (except for the first question) what questions you will be asked for each passage. Let's say you take the time to take detailed notes on each of three paragraphs in a passage, two of which are very technical and difficult to understand. Then you may only get asked detail-oriented questions from one of the paragraphs! All of that time would be wasted and impossible to recover. **If you find it helpful to jot down a few words for each paragraph, by all means do it, but detailed note taking will only hurt your pacing and accuracy.**

- **Be question-driven.** The difficulty in reading comp comes from the tricky, detail-oriented questions, which we will break down in detail in the next section. Most of the broad, Universal questions that you answer from your initial reading are the easy ones. As long as you get the information to answer those, you can save most of your time for finding information and connecting relevant details to answer Inference and Function questions. On these questions, if you are unsure of the answer, it usually means that you have not found the proper information in the passage. By budgeting your time wisely in the initial reading, you will have time to keep looking until you unlock the information or relationship required to answer the problem.

- **Go back to the passage for detail-oriented questions.** Resist the temptation to answer any detail-oriented question from your initial reading. Testmakers are clever about creating questions that punish people who do not specifically make sure that their answer is supported in the passage. Use your initial reading as a guide for detail-oriented questions, but always go back to specifically confirm your answer with something concrete from the passage. In Section 3 you will learn more specific strategies for this.

Now that we have summarized the STOP reading approach in detail, let's practice the reading approach with one passage and then look at a collection of Universal-type questions that you must be able to answer from that initial reading.

LESSON

Passage 1

Young Enterprise Services (YES) is a federal program created to encourage entrepreneurship in 14- to 18-year-olds who have already shown a clear aptitude for starting business ventures. The program, started in 2002, has provided loans, grants, and counseling—in the form of workshops and individual meetings with established entrepreneurs—to over 7500 young people. The future of YES, however, is now in jeopardy. A number of damaging criticisms have been leveled at the program, and members of the congressional agency that provides the funding have suggested that YES may be scaled down or even dismantled entirely.

One complaint is that the funds that YES distributes have disproportionally gone to young people from economically disadvantaged families, despite the program's stated goal of being blind to any criteria besides merit. Though no one has claimed that any of the recipients of YES funds have been undeserving, several families have brought lawsuits claiming that their requests for funding were rejected because of the families' relatively high levels of income. The resulting publicity was an embarrassment to the YES administrators, one of whom resigned.

Another challenge has been the admittedly difficult task of ensuring that a young person, not his or her family, is truly the driving force behind a venture. The rules state that the business plan must be created by the youth, and that any profits in excess of $1,000 be placed in an escrow account that can only be used for education, investment in the venture, and little else, for a period that is determined by the age of the recipient. Despite this, several grants had to be returned after it was discovered that parents—or in one case, a neighbor—were misusing YES funds to promote their own business ideas. To make matters worse, the story of the returned monies was at first denied by a YES spokesperson who then had to retract the denial, leading to more bad press.

In truth, YES has had some real success stories. A 14-year-old girl in Texas used the knowledge and funding she received through the program to connect with a distributor who now carries her line of custom-designed cell phone covers. Two brothers in Alaska have developed an online travel advisory service for young people vacationing with their families. Both of these ventures are profitable, and both companies have gained a striking amount of brand recognition in a very short time. However, YES has been pitifully lax in trumpeting these encouraging stories. Local press notwithstanding, these and other successes have received little media coverage. This is a shame, but one that can be remedied. The administrators of YES should heed the advice given in one of the program's own publications: "No business venture, whatever its appeal, will succeed for long without an active approach to public relations."

Applying STOP Strategy

Before you look at four broad questions relating to scope, tone, organization, and purpose, you should first summarize the passage based on the three important STOP questions:

1. What type of passage is this?

2. What are the broad topics of each paragraph?

3. What is the primary purpose?

To get a better idea of how to contend with implicit Universal questions, consider each component of STOP and questions you might see related to each.

Scope of the Passage

In order to properly identify the author's primary Purpose, you need to understand the Scope of the passage. Any test-taker can determine the general topic of a passage after a cursory look; the Scope of the passage is far subtler. Scope gives boundaries to the passage.

Imagine, for example, that economics is the general topic of a passage. That knowledge alone is fairly useless, since the test-makers will never ask such a general question. The Scope of the passage, however, is far more important. You might face a question about duopolies, so you need to know if that is within the confines of the passage's Scope.

Topic: Business Education

Subtopic: Entrepreneurship Programs

Scope: The YES program, its recent criticisms, and need for change

The example below illustrates the importance of Scope using the passage on page 24.

1. Which of the following would be the most appropriate title for this passage?

   (A) "Recent Difficulties in the YES Program"

   (B) "Federal Entrepreneurship Programs for Young Adults"

   (C) "Successes of the YES Program"

   (D) "Common Challenges Facing Federal Programs"

   (E) "The YES Program: How to Overcome Recent Challenges"

LESSON

LEARNING BY DOING
Scope Is the Key for Primary Purpose

Before analyzing the scope specifically, you should first answer the three STOP questions from the previous page:

1. What type of passage is this? → This is an opinionated passage. The author gives relatively strong opinion, evidenced by words such as "pitifully lax," "this is a shame," and "YES should…."

2. What are the broad topics of each paragraph? → The first paragraph introduces the YES program and the fact that it is in trouble. The second and third paragraphs detail some of the problems and criticisms of YES. The fourth paragraph, which is the most important in the passage, highlights several successes of YES, and gives the author's opinion about the program and what should be done to fix it.

3. What is the primary purpose? → The primary purpose of the passage is to present the author's opinion about how to save the program.

As you have already learned, scope is mainly important in how it relates to the primary purpose. This question about the most appropriate title (another way to present primary purpose) is no exception. In answering any primary purpose question, you must pick the answer choice that captures the entire passage, not just some part of it. Most incorrect answer choices on primary purpose questions are too narrow in scope and some are too broad. Answer choice A is too narrow in scope and leaves out the all-important fourth paragraph: The goal of this passage is not to highlight the difficulties, but rather to highlight the author's opinion of how to fix it. Answer choice C is also too narrow, as the successes are just a small part of the fourth paragraph. Answer choices B and D are both way too broad; this passage is about the specifics of the YES program, not about federal programs in general. Answer choice E has the proper topic and scope; the passage is about the YES program and the author's ideas for how to overcome recent difficulties.

THINK LIKE THE TESTMAKER
Misdirection

On almost every primary purpose question, you will see at least one answer choice that is exactly about some portion of the passage. For instance, in this problem you spent two paragraphs reading about some difficulties of the YES program, so it would be easy to pick answer choice A, the classic "too narrow" sucker choice. Testmakers are good at guiding you to an answer choice that is correct for half the passage but not for the whole passage. Often the correct answer, which does get the scope correct, will be hidden behind convoluted language so that you are hesitant to pick it. Focus on scope and you will avoid falling for this trap.

The Author's Tone

Tone is an important component to any passage and relates directly to the type of passage. If the passage is explanatory/descriptive, then the goal of that passage is to explain and/or describe something, not to present opinion. There may be "accidental" tone—some portion might contain an opinion of the author that was not intended— but it is not the purpose of the passage. If the passage is analytical, the purpose of the passage is to analyze some topic or event. The passage will typically not contain overt tone, but it will be subjective in nature and suggestive in tone. If the passage is opinionated, the purpose of the passage is to present an opinion or a hypothesis. While portions of the passage might be explanatory/descriptive, those parts are only serving as a set-up for the author's opinion or hypothesis.

While reading any passage, you should look carefully for important trigger words that indicate tone. If there is tone in a passage, then typically at least one question will hinge upon your recognition of that tone. Consider an example problem from this passage:

LESSON

Passage 1

Young Enterprise Services (YES) is a federal program created to encourage entrepreneurship in 14- to 18-year-olds who have already shown a clear aptitude for starting business ventures. The program, started in 2002, has provided loans, grants, and counseling—in the form of workshops and individual meetings with established entrepreneurs—to over 7500 young people. The future of YES, however, is now in jeopardy. A number of damaging criticisms have been leveled at the program, and members of the congressional agency that provides the funding have suggested that YES may be scaled down or even dismantled entirely.

One complaint is that the funds that YES distributes have disproportionally gone to young people from economically disadvantaged families, despite the program's stated goal of being blind to any criteria besides merit. Though no one has claimed that any of the recipients of YES funds have been undeserving, several families have brought lawsuits claiming that their requests for funding were rejected because of the families' relatively high levels of income. The resulting publicity was an embarrassment to the YES administrators, one of whom resigned.

Another challenge has been the admittedly difficult task of ensuring that a young person, not his or her family, is truly the driving force behind a venture. The rules state that the business plan must be created by the youth, and that any profits in excess of $1,000 be placed in an escrow account that can only be used for education, investment in the venture, and little else, for a period that is determined by the age of the recipient. Despite this, several grants had to be returned after it was discovered that parents— or in one case, a neighbor—were misusing YES funds to promote their own business ideas. To make matters worse, the story of the returned monies was at first denied by a YES spokesperson who then had to retract the denial, leading to more bad press.

In truth, YES has had some real success stories. A 14-year-old girl in Texas used the knowledge and funding she received through the program to connect with a distributor who now carries her line of custom-designed cell phone covers. Two brothers in Alaska have developed an online travel advisory service for young people vacationing with their families. Both of these ventures are profitable, and both companies have gained a striking amount of brand recognition in a very short time. However, YES has been pitifully lax in trumpeting these encouraging stories. Local press notwithstanding, these and other successes have received little media coverage. This is a shame, but one that can be remedied. The administrators of YES should heed the advice given in one of the program's own publications: "No business venture, whatever its appeal, will succeed for long without an active approach to public relations."

2. The author of the passage would most likely describe YES as a _____.

    (A) failed enterprise that is beyond repair

    (B) noble effort that has been hampered by external factors

    (C) limited success that can be improved through greater fiscal responsibility

    (D) potentially worthy program that has been mismanaged

    (E) waste of public resources that should never have received funding

LESSON

LEARNING BY DOING
Focus on Tone Whenever it Is Present

For the first three paragraphs, this passage seems to be explanatory/ descriptive, but then in the fourth paragraph fairly strong tone appears. When you see trigger words such as "pitifully lax," "this is a shame," and "YES should…," you are sure the passage is opinionated. Whenever you see trigger words for tone, you should slow down and make sure you understand clearly the author's opinion. Here, that opinion is this: While the YES program has problems, the program is actually quite successful, and the administrators need to do a better job trumpeting those success stories.

Given the fairly positive view of the program by the author, answer choices A and E could never be correct. The author does not like the way the administrators are handling public relations, but overall he views the program as worthy. Words like "failed" and "waste" do not match the tone of the passage. "Noble effort" and "limited success" in answer choices B and C do match the tone of the author, so you must read those carefully. From your initial reading, it is essential that you understand the major problem that YES is facing: its internal handling of public relations. So while answer choices B and C match the tone, they incorrectly describe the problem: It is not fiscal responsibility, and the factors affecting it are not external. Answer choice D captures both the tone ("potentially worthy program") and the topic ("public relations have been mismanaged") properly and is thus correct.

SKILLS MEET STRATEGY
Look for Important Transitions

One common trait of GMAT Reading Comprehension passages is that they often contain abrupt transitions. These transitions create problems for people who try to read too quickly, as you could easily miss them in your initial reading. In this passage, that important transition takes place in the middle of the fourth paragraph. The passage goes from a benign description of the YES program and some recent problems to a strongly opinionated portion in which the author presents his suggestion and views. Strong transitions are an important part of GMAT passages, so make sure you look for trigger words that indicate tone or any change within the passage.

Organization

Paying particular attention to Organization helps address two common difficulties: losing focus (particularly while reading lengthy or very technical passages) and missing the main Purpose by overlooking the direction of the author's argument. Immediately after reading each paragraph, stop briefly and ask yourself the point of that paragraph in the passage overall. Use the acronym STOP to help yourself remember. By doing so, you can hold yourself accountable for constant concentration—and quickly recognize and remedy any lapses in focus. Considering the point of each paragraph will help you build a step-by-step understanding of the passage as you progress through it. Understanding the Organization will also give you a mental road map; this mental table of contents will enable you to quickly find the information relevant to questions on specific facts or concepts.

Take note of wording that signals Organization; signal wording can help you understand not only the Scope, but also the direction and perspective of the author's argument. Often, one or two words in each paragraph signal either a transition (however, but, or in contrast) or a continuation/expansion (moreover, similarly, or second). The wording listed on the right-hand page often signals Organization; be sensitive to such wording, as it can help reveal the Scope, Tone, and Purpose. Use this information in order to correctly answer the example that follows.

Premise	Continuation/ Expansion	Soft Transition	Strong Transition	Conclusion	Opposition
Because	Additionally	Admittedly	Alternatively	As a result	Against
Evidence	Also	Assumption	Although	Certainly	Argue
For example	Another	Consider	But	Consequently	Cast doubt
For instance	Common	Distinction	By contrast	Hence	Claim
Illustrated by	Especially	Even	Can be argued	Implies	Contend
In fact	Furthermore	Exception	Conversely	Inference	Contrary
In reality	Indeed	Granted	Despite	In essence	Deny
Since	In addition	In any case	Difference	In short	Refuse
	In turn	In part	However	In summary	Wrong
	Just as	New	In contrast	Must be true	
	Moreover	Not complete	In spite of	Obviously	
	Second	Now	Instead	Therefore	
	Shared	On one hand	Nevertheless	Thus	
	Similarly	Question	On the other hand	Undeniably	
	Third	Still	Rather than	Undoubtedly	
	Too	Surprising	Though		
		To be sure	Yet		
		While			

LESSON

Passage 1

Young Enterprise Services (YES) is a federal program created to encourage entrepreneurship in 14- to 18-year-olds who have already shown a clear aptitude for starting business ventures. The program, started in 2002, has provided loans, grants, and counseling—in the form of workshops and individual meetings with established entrepreneurs—to over 7500 young people. The future of YES, however, is now in jeopardy. A number of damaging criticisms have been leveled at the program, and members of the congressional agency that provides the funding have suggested that YES may be scaled down or even dismantled entirely.

One complaint is that the funds that YES distributes have disproportionally gone to young people from economically disadvantaged families, despite the program's stated goal of being blind to any criteria besides merit. Though no one has claimed that any of the recipients of YES funds have been undeserving, several families have brought lawsuits claiming that their requests for funding were rejected because of the families' relatively high levels of income. The resulting publicity was an embarrassment to the YES administrators, one of whom resigned.

Another challenge has been the admittedly difficult task of ensuring that a young person, not his or her family, is truly the driving force behind a venture. The rules state that the business plan must be created by the youth, and that any profits in excess of $1,000 be placed in an escrow account that can only be used for education, investment in the venture, and little else, for a period that is determined by the age of the recipient. Despite this, several grants had to be returned after it was discovered that parents— or in one case, a neighbor—were misusing YES funds to promote their own business ideas. To make matters worse, the story of the returned monies was at first denied by a YES spokesperson who then had to retract the denial, leading to more bad press.

In truth, YES has had some real success stories. A 14-year-old girl in Texas used the knowledge and funding she received through the program to connect with a distributor who now carries her line of custom-designed cell phone covers. Two brothers in Alaska have developed an online travel advisory service for young people vacationing with their families. Both of these ventures are profitable, and both companies have gained a striking amount of brand recognition in a very short time. However, YES has been pitifully lax in trumpeting these encouraging stories. Local press notwithstanding, these and other successes have received little media coverage. This is a shame, but one that can be remedied. The administrators of YES should heed the advice given in one of the program's own publications: "No business venture, whatever its appeal, will succeed for long without an active approach to public relations."

3. All of the following are discussed in the passage except _____.

    (A) the resignation of some YES administrators

    (B) bad press resulting from financial improprieties

    (C) lawsuits against YES

    (D) the YES program's stated goals

    (E) current levels of YES funding

LEARNING BY DOING
Use Organization as a Guide

One of the most important attributes of the STOP strategy is that it keeps you focused on the overall structure. **REMEMBER: After every paragraph, you should stop and take a mental note of the topic and role of the paragraph you have just read**. This focus on organization will help you on all Reading Comprehension questions, because you will be more efficient in gauging scope, and you will know where to look for specific information. Some questions, such as this one, are testing organization and structure explicitly; they reward those who can find information within the passage quickly. From your initial reading, you should have noted the structure highlighted previously:

The first paragraph introduces the YES program and the fact that it is in trouble. The second and third paragraphs detail some of the problems and criticisms of YES. The fourth paragraph, which is the most important in the passage, highlights several successes of YES, and gives the author's opinion about the program and what should be done to fix it.

Since answer choices A, B, and C all relate to potential problems that you might have read about, you should look for them in the second and third paragraphs. "The resignation of administrators can be found" on line 15, "bad press resulting from financial improprieties" can be found on line 24, and "lawsuits against YES" can be found on line 13. Since answer choices D and E relate to the program more generally, it is likely that you will find them in the introductory paragraph, in which the program is summarized. The stated goals are given in the first sentence, but there is no information given about "current levels of funding," so answer choice E is correct.

Purpose

If there is one question stem you are certain to see on the GMAT, it is:

The primary purpose of the passage is

The Purpose is similar to a thesis statement from a term paper. However, if the author's Purpose was readily apparent, the test makers would not be able to ask any questions about it (they would be far too easy to answer). Instead, the test makers give you passages that contain main ideas buried in inscrutable writing or obscure terminology. Thankfully, once you find the Purpose, it is rarely hard to understand.

In reading GMAT passages, determining the author's Purpose is ultimately your most important goal. Use your understanding of the Scope, Tone, and Organization to help guide you to the Purpose. The relationship between these elements is depicted in the diagram below, and followed by an example question using the same passage as before.

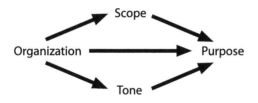

Passage 1

Young Enterprise Services (YES) is a federal program created to encourage entrepreneurship in 14- to 18-year-olds who have already shown a clear aptitude for starting business ventures. The program, started in 2002, has provided loans, grants, and counseling—in the form of workshops and individual meetings with established entrepreneurs—to over 7500 young people. The future of YES, however, is now in jeopardy. A number of damaging criticisms have been leveled at the program, and members of the congressional agency that provides the funding have suggested that YES may be scaled down or even dismantled entirely.

One complaint is that the funds that YES distributes have disproportionally gone to young people from economically disadvantaged families, despite the program's stated goal of being blind to any criteria besides merit. Though no one has claimed that any of the recipients of YES funds have been undeserving, several families have brought lawsuits claiming that their requests for funding were rejected because of the families' relatively high levels of income. The resulting publicity was an embarrassment to the YES administrators, one of whom resigned.

Another challenge has been the admittedly difficult task of ensuring that a young person, not his or her family, is truly the driving force behind a venture. The rules state that the business plan must be created by the youth, and that any profits in excess of $1,000 be placed in an escrow account that can only be used for education, investment in the venture, and little else, for a period that is determined by the age of the recipient. Despite this, several grants had to be returned after it was discovered that parents— or in one case, a neighbor—were misusing YES funds to promote their own business ideas. To make matters worse, the story of the returned monies was at first denied by a YES spokesperson who then had to retract the denial, leading to more bad press.

In truth, YES has had some real success stories. A 14-year-old girl in Texas used the knowledge and funding she received through the program to connect with a distributor who now carries her line of custom-designed cell phone covers. Two brothers in Alaska have developed an online travel advisory service for young people vacationing with their families. Both of these ventures are profitable, and both companies have gained a striking amount of brand recognition in a very short time. However, YES has been pitifully lax in trumpeting these encouraging stories. Local press notwithstanding, these and other successes have received little media coverage. This is a shame, but one that can be remedied. The administrators of YES should heed the advice given in one of the program's own publications: "No business venture, whatever its appeal, will succeed for long without an active approach to public relations."

4. The primary purpose of the passage is to _____.

(A) detail the approach that should be taken in remedying YES's public relations problems

(B) defend YES from the various criticisms that have been leveled against it

(C) suggest a way to improve the program

(D) detail several criticisms and problems of the YES program

(E) make the case that YES, despite some difficulties, has been quite successful for some people who have taken part in the program

LEARNING BY DOING
Primary Purpose Is About Scope and Passage Type

Earlier in this section, you learned how important scope is for determining the primary purpose. This, of course, still holds true on this question, and it should be no surprise that several of the answer choices are too narrow in scope. Answer choices D and E both describe sections of the passage, but they leave out the all-important opinion and prescription of the author. Answer choice A is off topic and out of scope. The author does not specifically detail the approach that should be taken; he only says that the public relations should be changed. With answer choice B, the author is not defending YES against the criticisms, but rather showing that there are successes that should be highlighted. Answer choice C perfectly captures the primary purpose: to give the author's opinion about how to save YES. Many people are hesitant to pick answer choice C because it seems to leave out the first three paragraphs, but remember that the first three paragraphs are only there as set-up for the final all-important paragraph. The correct answer choice is C.

SKILLS MEET STRATEGY
Focus on the First Word or Phrase in Answer Choices

Another important component of primary purpose questions relates to the first word or phrase of the answer choices. Most answer choices in these questions start with a verb that must properly match the passage type. In this problem the five verbs or verb phrases are "detail," "defend," "suggest," "detail," and "make the case." This passage is opinionated, so it is unlikely that the primary purpose could be simply to detail something; that would likely only match an explanatory/descriptive passage. However, "defend," "suggest," and "make the case" all relate to presenting an opinion, so they are more likely to be correct. **REMEMBER:** You should always read all answer choices, but the first signal word could disqualify an answer choice quickly if it does not match the passage type.

STOP Reading Strategy Summary

The STOP strategy permits you to read each passage efficiently in a way that saves time and sets you up for success on the questions that follow. To read for STOP, you should:

- Stop at the end of each paragraph to note, in five to seven words (if you write anything at all), what the paragraph is about (scope) and why it was written (organization).

- At the end of the passage, ask yourself three questions:
  1. What type of passage was it?
  2. What was the organization of each paragraph?
  3. What was the primary purpose?

STOP also serves to help you re-focus if you ever feel as though you simply cannot engage with a passage. If that happens, shift your full attention to organization, scanning for transitional language to build your understanding of the direction of the passage.

When students struggle with reading comprehension it is usually because they take too long to read, they focus too deeply on the details, or they take too many notes. Let STOP be your guide for reading at the proper level and for gleaning the necessary takeaways from each passage so that you can attack the questions, which are covered in the next section.

LESSON

SECTION 3: MASTERING THE COMMON QUESTION TYPES

The directions on the Reading Comprehension section of the GMAT ask you to "choose the best answer to each question," but what the testmakers really mean is to "choose the only correct answer to each question." If evidence in a passage supported two or more answer choices, it would be unfair to test-takers. GMAC is reluctant to withdraw questions, so they try to design every question on the GMAT to have only one supportable answer choice (even if that answer is not immediately obvious).

Understanding this is the key to doing well on Reading Comprehension (especially on detail-oriented questions): There must be evidence in the passage to support one and only one choice, but it is often hard to find! The difficulty is often finding that information, particularly given the time pressures on the test overall. **Generally speaking in reading comprehension, if you are picking an answer choice because it seems correct and not because you have found a concrete piece of evidence in the passage, it is the sucker choice.** If you find the cleverly hidden piece of information and/or relationship in the passage, you are generally sure that you are getting it correct (and you will recognize the tempting sucker choice).

As you learned earlier, there are two broad types of questions:

1. **Implicit Universal questions** that ask about broader concepts in the passage. These should be answered from your initial reading (although you might have to peek back sometimes) and are generally easier. They are, however, more obtuse and are not necessarily supported by one or two specific statements within the passage.

2. **Explicit detail-oriented questions** that ask about specific information and/ or relationships within the passage. These are often more cleverly made, but can almost always be supported by an explicit (but cleverly hidden) piece of information or relationship within the passage.

LESSON

In the previous section, you learned how to contend with many of the Universal questions and how to read properly to answer those questions. You will see one of those at the end of this section, but the primary goal of this section is to teach you how to succeed on the detail-oriented questions. Overall, there are four important categories of Reading Comp questions:

1. **Inference**
2. **Specific**
3. **Function**
4. **Universal**

Before you see detailed strategies for each type, it is essential to consider several broad strategies that apply to all types. These are highlighted on the next page:

General Strategies for Reading Comprehension Questions

- **Don't rely on outside knowledge of a topic.** Many questions are designed so that one of the answer choices is a completely reasonable statement based on your knowledge of the topic at hand, but it is not supported by the passage. This is one of the most common tricks used by testmakers to make hard problems. Knowledge of a topic will help you read the passage more effectively (you will be engaged and understand the topic better), but be careful that you do not use that knowledge to answer questions.

- **Look for concrete evidence.** Almost every explicit, detail-oriented question has definitive support somewhere in the passage. Remember: If you are answering a detail-oriented question based on a gut feeling or your knowledge of a topic, it is almost surely the incorrect sucker choice. Except for Universal questions, almost all Reading Comprehension questions are based on concrete evidence.

- **Know where to look in the passage.** If you use the STOP reading strategy properly, you will have a general idea about the topic of each paragraph. Use important key words in the question stem or in the answer choices to guide you back to the passage. **Finding the proper information quickly is essential to success in Reading Comprehension.**

- **Some questions are just easy.** On most of the GMAT, if an answer choice is relatively obvious, it is almost surely a sucker choice! However, in reading comprehension there are a surprising number of straightforward questions. Don't be hesitant to pick a seemingly easy answer choice, as long as you have found concrete support for it within the passage. These straightforward questions can be most problematic for "sophisticated" test-takers, as they will often overthink Reading Comprehension questions.

- **Be on the lookout for wordplay and misdirection.** These common tricks used by testmakers in critical reasoning are everywhere in reading comprehension. For instance, just because an answer choice mentions several words from one part of the passage, don't assume that it is correct. Testmakers are expert at creating answer choices that are similar to what you have read in the passage, but actually contradict what is there or go beyond the stated information.

- **Stay within the boundaries of the passage.** Most difficult Reading Comp questions share one important quality with Critical Reasoning Inference questions: They entice you to go a little too far with your conclusion. Don't be tempted to go too far, and stay within the boundaries of the stated information in the passage.

Keep those strategies in mind throughout this section and in your own preparation. Testmakers play the same game over and over in reading comp, and pattern recognition is key in your preparation. On the next page is a passage followed by one example of each type of question. The specific strategies for each type will he highlighted with each question.

LESSON

Nearly all the workers of the Lowell textile mills of Massachusetts were unmarried daughters from farm families. Some of the workers were as young as 10. Since many people in the 1820s were disturbed by the idea of working females, the company provided well-kept dormitories and boardinghouses. The meals were decent and church attendance was mandatory. Compared to other factories of the time, the Lowell mills were clean and safe, and there was even a journal, *The Lowell Offering*, which contained poems and other material written by the workers, and which became known beyond New England. Ironically, it was at the Lowell mills that dissatisfaction with working conditions brought about the first organization of working women.

The mills were highly mechanized, and were in fact considered a model of efficiency by others in the textile industry. The work was difficult, however, and the high level of standardization made it tedious. When wages were cut, the workers organized the Factory Girls Association. 15,000 women decided to "turn out," or walk off the job. *The Offering*, meant as a pleasant creative outlet, gave the women a voice that could be heard by sympathetic people elsewhere in the country, and even in Europe. However, the ability of the women to demand changes was severely circumscribed by an inability to go for long without wages with which to support themselves and help support their families. This same limitation hampered the effectiveness of the Lowell Female Labor Reform Association (LFLRA), organized in 1844.

No specific reform can be directly attributed to the Lowell workers, but their legacy is unquestionable. The LFLRA's founder, Sarah Bagley, became a national figure, testifying before the Massachusetts House of Representatives. When the New England Labor Reform League was formed, three of the eight board members were women. Other mill workers took note of the Lowell strikes, and were successful in getting better pay, shorter hours, and safer working conditions. Even some existing child labor laws can be traced back to efforts first set in motion by the Lowell mills women.

STOP Reading Summary
1. What type of passage is this?
2. What are the broad topics of each paragraph?
3. What is the primary purpose?

1. *This is a classic example of an analytical passage. It is subjective in the final paragraph and goes beyond being simply explanatory/descriptive with the following sentence: "No specific reform can be directly attributed to the Lowell workers, but their legacy is unquestionable."*

2. *The first paragraph describes the working conditions at the Lowell mills and notes that it was the first place where working women organized to express their dissatisfaction. The second paragraph describes how the women organized and some of the difficulties they faced. The third paragraph is subjective and relates the Lowell mills to the labor reform movement as a whole.*

3. *The primary purpose of this passage is to highlight the importance of the Lowell mill strikes to the broader labor reform movement.*

Specific

Specific questions ask about the details of a passage. Your task here is to locate the pertinent portion of the passage and click the answer choice that contains the relevant details. Specific questions are logically identical to Inference questions from critical reasoning: The answer must be true according to the passage. Most commonly, the correct answer will be a simple paraphrase of part of the passage. Make sure that you answer the question asked; there may be some answer choices that are true according to the passage, but are not relevant to the question at hand.

Nearly all the workers of the Lowell textile mills of Massachusetts were unmarried daughters from farm families. Some of the workers were as young as 10. Since many people in the 1820s were disturbed by the idea of working females, the company provided well-kept dormitories and boardinghouses. The meals were decent and church attendance was mandatory. Compared to other factories of the time, the Lowell mills were clean and safe, and there was even a journal, *The Lowell Offering*, which contained poems and other material written by the workers, and which became known beyond New England. Ironically, it was at the Lowell mills that dissatisfaction with working conditions brought about the first organization of working women.

The mills were highly mechanized, and were in fact considered a model of efficiency by others in the textile industry. The work was difficult, however, and the high level of standardization made it tedious. When wages were cut, the workers organized the Factory Girls Association. 15,000 women decided to "turn out," or walk off the job. *The Offering*, meant as a pleasant creative outlet, gave the women a voice that could be heard by sympathetic people elsewhere in the country, and even in Europe. However, the ability of the women to demand changes was severely circumscribed by an inability to go for long without wages with which to support themselves and help support their families. This same limitation hampered the effectiveness of the Lowell Female Labor Reform Association (LFLRA), organized in 1844.

No specific reform can be directly attributed to the Lowell workers, but their legacy is unquestionable. The LFLRA's founder, Sarah Bagley, became a national figure, testifying before the Massachusetts House of Representatives. When the New England Labor Reform League was formed, three of the eight board members were women. Other mill workers took note of the Lowell strikes, and were successful in getting better pay, shorter hours, and safer working conditions. Even some existing child labor laws can be traced back to efforts first set in motion by the Lowell mills women.

5. According to the passage, which of the following contributed to the inability of the workers at Lowell to have their demands met?

   (A) The very young age of some of the workers made political organization impractical.

   (B) Social attitudes of the time pressured women into not making demands.

   (C) The Lowell Female Labor Reform Association was not organized until 1844.

   (D) Their families depended on the workers to send some of their wages home.

   (E) The people who were most sympathetic to the workers lived outside of New England.

"According to the passage" is by far the most common key phrase in Specific questions.

Other Examples of Specific Questions:

- The passage warns of which of the following dangers?

- The author of the passage mentions which of the following as an example of X?

- The author cites each of the following as influences on X EXCEPT....

LESSON

LEARNING BY DOING
Correct Answers Are Often Just Rephrasing Something in the Passage

Specific questions are very common in reading comprehension. To answer them, you must quickly find the relevant information in the passage and then pick the answer choice that is simply rephrasing what is there. It is important to note, however, that these are not always as simple as they sound. Sometimes the information is cleverly hidden within the passage, and often the rephrasing is so tricky that you do not realize that the answer choice is the same as what you read in the passage. With technical passages in particular, you should be careful with Specific questions, as the correct answer is often a clever rephrasing of some technical process.

On this question, the process is relatively straightforward, as the question stem is quite specific. From your STOP summary, you know that the required information should be in the second paragraph, because that is where the strikes and accompanying difficulties were discussed. Line 16 gives you almost verbatim evidence for answer choice D, so you know it's correct. The other answer choices are not supported at all in the passage and as a result this is a relatively straightforward specific question.

THINK LIKE THE TESTMAKER
Misdirection

Generally speaking, Specific questions are easier than Inference questions (which you will learn about next) because you do not have to actually infer or conclude anything. In practice, however, testmakers can use this against you. The following is a very common set-up on technical passages: Testmakers give you an "according to the passage" question in which the correct answer is a clever rewording of some technical process. It is a Specific-type question, but they bait you into thinking you must make an inference. The incorrect sucker choice(s) will be more satisfying, because you seem to have made some clever inference, but those inferences will be incorrect. Often they are reasonable inferences, but ones that are not supported by the passage, and other times they are simply not supported by the material. Regardless, don't forget that many questions simply regurgitate what is written. **Sometimes you should not infer, just regurgitate, especially on technical science passages!**

Inference

Inference questions ask you to draw a conclusion based on evidence from the passage (i.e., what **must be true** based on the passage). They are logically identical to Critical Reasoning Inference questions but can be more difficult because the required information might be hard to find and/or located in several different places within the passage. Specific and Inference questions are logically identical in that the answer you pick must be true. The difference is that for Inference questions you must do more than simply regurgitate what is there. Regardless, remember that the correct answer must be true; that is what matters in the end. For instance, if a question asks "What you can logically infer from the passage?" do not be afraid to pick something that is simply paraphrasing a statement in the passage. It must be true and is thus the correct answer.

LESSON

Nearly all the workers of the Lowell textile mills of Massachusetts were unmarried daughters from farm families. Some of the workers were as young as 10. Since many people in the 1820s were disturbed by the idea of working females, the company provided well-kept dormitories and boardinghouses. The meals were decent and church attendance was mandatory. Compared to other factories of the time, the Lowell mills were clean and safe, and there was even a journal, *The Lowell Offering*, which contained poems and other material written by the workers, and which became known beyond New England. Ironically, it was at the Lowell mills that dissatisfaction with working conditions brought about the first organization of working women.

The mills were highly mechanized, and were in fact considered a model of efficiency by others in the textile industry. The work was difficult, however, and the high level of standardization made it tedious. When wages were cut, the workers organized the Factory Girls Association. 15,000 women decided to "turn out," or walk off the job. *The Offering*, meant as a pleasant creative outlet, gave the women a voice that could be heard by sympathetic people elsewhere in the country, and even in Europe. However, the ability of the women to demand changes was severely circumscribed by an inability to go for long without wages with which to support themselves and help support their families. This same limitation hampered the effectiveness of the Lowell Female Labor Reform Association (LFLRA), organized in 1844.

No specific reform can be directly attributed to the Lowell workers, but their legacy is unquestionable. The LFLRA's founder, Sarah Bagley, became a national figure, testifying before the Massachusetts House of Representatives. When the New England Labor Reform League was formed, three of the eight board members were women. Other mill workers took note of the Lowell strikes, and were successful in getting better pay, shorter hours, and safer working conditions. Even some existing child labor laws can be traced back to efforts first set in motion by the Lowell mills women.

6. The author of the passage implies that the efforts of the women workers at the Lowell mills _____.

    (A) were of less direct benefit to them than to other workers

    (B) led to the creation of child labor laws that benefited the youngest workers at the Lowell mills

    (C) forced the New England Labor Reform League to include three women on its board

    (D) were addressed in the poetry included in The Offering

    (E) were initially organized by Sarah Bagley

Other Examples of Inference Questions Include:

- The author would most likely agree with which of the following statements?

- It can be inferred from the passage that….

LESSON

LEARNING BY DOING
Leveraging Information

Inference questions are the most difficult when you have to leverage and connect separate pieces of information within a passage. This question is a perfect example of leveraging two pieces of information: 1. In line 15 (and from the previous question) you learn that the women of the Lowell strikes could not reap any benefits because they had to go back to work to support their families. 2. In line 24 you learn that "other mill workers took note of the Lowell strikes and were successful in getting better pay," etc. From those two statements you can infer that the efforts of the women workers "were of less direct benefit to them than to other workers," so answer choice A is correct.

It is important to note how much subtler this is than either a "just regurgitate" Specific question or an Inference question in which you need to only use one piece of information. You cannot make this inference from either statement alone, but with both it must be true. The difficulty lies in both finding and linking those pieces of together in order to recognize that answer choice A must be true. Several of the other inferences are close (especially answer choice D), but they all go a little too far and make statements that cannot be concretely supported by the passage.

Function

Function questions ask you why—why an author included certain evidence or wording, or why he arranged the evidence in a particular way. Answering these questions depends almost entirely on context. The answer will not lie in the statement itself but in the words surrounding and/or leading up to it. This is the major difference between Function and Specific/Inference questions: With Specific/Inference questions, the answer usually lies in the statements themselves and how they are linked or how they are repackaged. For Function questions, you must look at the bigger picture and why a statement exists in some context. Try the following Function question on the Lowell mills passage:

Nearly all the workers of the Lowell textile mills of Massachusetts were unmarried daughters from farm families. Some of the workers were as young as 10. Since many people in the 1820s were disturbed by the idea of working females, the company provided well-kept dormitories and boardinghouses. The meals were decent and church attendance was mandatory. Compared to other factories of the time, the Lowell mills were clean and safe, and there was even a journal, *The Lowell Offering*, which contained poems and other material written by the workers, and which became known beyond New England. Ironically, it was at the Lowell mills that dissatisfaction with working conditions brought about the first organization of working women.

The mills were highly mechanized, and were in fact considered a model of efficiency by others in the textile industry. The work was difficult, however, and the high level of standardization made it tedious. When wages were cut, the workers organized the Factory Girls Association. 15,000 women decided to "turn out," or walk off the job. *The Offering*, meant as a pleasant creative outlet, gave the women a voice that could be heard by sympathetic people elsewhere in the country, and even in Europe. However, the ability of the women to demand changes was severely circumscribed by an inability to go for long without wages with which to support themselves and help support their families. This same limitation hampered the effectiveness of the Lowell Female Labor Reform Association (LFLRA), organized in 1844.

No specific reform can be directly attributed to the Lowell workers, but their legacy is unquestionable. The LFLRA's founder, Sarah Bagley, became a national figure, testifying before the Massachusetts House of Representatives. When the New England Labor Reform League was formed, three of the eight board members were women. Other mill workers took note of the Lowell strikes, and were successful in getting better pay, shorter hours, and safer working conditions. Even some existing child labor laws can be traced back to efforts first set in motion by the Lowell mills women.

7. The author uses the word "Ironically" in the first paragraph to indicate that _____.

    (A) none of the people who ran the Lowell mills expected that the workers would organize to express dissatisfaction with working conditions

    (B) the women who worked at the Lowell mills did not realize how fortunate they were to work at such a place

    (C) it could be considered surprising that an early effort to demand better working conditions began in an environment that was especially designed to promote worker satisfaction

    (D) the people who created the working environment for the women at the Lowell mills did not really understand what it was they needed

    (E) it was unusual for women workers of the time to organize, regardless of their work environment

Other Examples of Function Questions:

*   "The author mentions X in order to…."

*   "One function of the second paragraph is to…."

*   "The discussion of X is meant to…."

*   "The author quotes X primarily in order to…."

LESSON

LEARNING BY DOING
It's All About the Context

This question, while not heroically difficult, is a perfect example of the Function question type. If you only read the sentence containing "ironically" you might guess why it's ironic, but you could never be sure. You need the context to understand completely why that word is there. If an entire paragraph is spent describing how good the working conditions are in a factory, and then at the end of that paragraph you learn that it is the first place where women held strikes, that defines ironic! Remember that ironic means "contrary to expectation," so you need the context to learn how or why it is contrary to expectation, and answer choice C explains it perfectly.

SKILLS MEET STRATEGY
Function Questions Are Like Boldface Critical Reasoning

Specific and Inference questions in reading comprehension are logically identical to Inference questions in critical reasoning: You must pick the only answer that must be true based on the information given. In Function questions you are focused much more on the role of a statement in the passage, and the thought process required is very similar to what you learned in Method of Reasoning (specifically the boldface type). Focus on context and make sure you are accurately describing the role in the correct answer. Also, remember that the GMAT is testing a set of integrated and overlapping skills; what you learn in preparation for one question type is often very important in another.

SKILLS MEET STRATEGY
Focus on the Main Point of the Paragraph

For most Function questions, the answer lies in the main point of the paragraph in which the information is found (rarely do you have to go out of that paragraph). If you understand the purpose of the paragraph (here to describe how good the working conditions are) then you can understand why an example or statement has been used. Any time you are asked about the role of a statement in a paragraph, think about your summary of that paragraph from your STOP analysis and how the statement relates to it.

Universal

Universal questions ask you to characterize the passage as a whole. The answers to Universal questions come directly from STOP; if you've correctly identified STOP, you won't need to look back at the passage. In fact, many Universal questions ask you directly for the Tone, Organization, or Purpose, just like the examples we studied in the first passage. As you have seen already, the most common type of Universal question is one that asks about the primary purpose.

Nearly all the workers of the Lowell textile mills of Massachusetts were unmarried daughters from farm families. Some of the workers were as young as 10. Since many people in the 1820s were disturbed by the idea of working females, the company provided well-kept dormitories and boardinghouses. The meals were decent and church attendance was mandatory. Compared to other factories of the time, the Lowell mills were clean and safe, and there was even a journal, *The Lowell Offering*, which contained poems and other material written by the workers, and which became known beyond New England. Ironically, it was at the Lowell mills that dissatisfaction with working conditions brought about the first organization of working women.

The mills were highly mechanized, and were in fact considered a model of efficiency by others in the textile industry. The work was difficult, however, and the high level of standardization made it tedious. When wages were cut, the workers organized the Factory Girls Association. 15,000 women decided to "turn out," or walk off the job. *The Offering*, meant as a pleasant creative outlet, gave the women a voice that could be heard by sympathetic people elsewhere in the country, and even in Europe. However, the ability of the women to demand changes was severely circumscribed by an inability to go for long without wages with which to support themselves and help support their families. This same limitation hampered the effectiveness of the Lowell Female Labor Reform Association (LFLRA), organized in 1844.

No specific reform can be directly attributed to the Lowell workers, but their legacy is unquestionable. The LFLRA's founder, Sarah Bagley, became a national figure, testifying before the Massachusetts House of Representatives. When the New England Labor Reform League was formed, three of the eight board members were women. Other mill workers took note of the Lowell strikes, and were successful in getting better pay, shorter hours, and safer working conditions. Even some existing child labor laws can be traced back to efforts first set in motion by the Lowell mills women.

8.   The primary purpose of the passage is to do which of the following?

   (A) Describe the labor reforms that can be attributed to the workers at the Lowell mills

   (B) Criticize the proprietors of the Lowell mills for their labor practices

   (C) Suggest that the Lowell mills played a large role in the labor reform movement

   (D) Describe the conditions under which the Lowell mills employees worked

   (E) Analyze the business practices of early American factories

Other Examples of Universal Questions:

•   "The passage is most relevant to which of the following areas of study?"

•   "The author of the passage is primarily concerned with…."

•   "Which of the following best describes the organization of the passage?"

LESSON

LEARNING BY DOING
For Primary Purpose, It's Always the Same Tricks

At this point in the lesson, you have been well trained in how to approach primary purpose questions. You need to focus on scope, and you need to make sure that the active verb in the answer choices matches the passage type. In this example, that approach allows you to immediately eliminate answer choice B: "Criticize" is way too strong of a word for an analytical piece. The other verbs are appropriate, so you should turn to scope. Answer choice D is too narrow in scope, as that refers only to the first paragraph, and answer choice E is way too broad (and off topic), as this passage is only about the effects of the Lowell mill strikes. Answer choice A is directly contradicted by line 20, so you are left to pick answer choice C, which properly matches the passage type ("suggest" is perfect for an analytical context) and the scope (the third paragraph is the most important; it is the role of the Lowell mill strikes that matter in the passage).

SKILLS MEET STRATEGY
Pattern Recognition

As you will see in your preparation, testmakers use the same tricks over and over again in reading comp. This is particularly true with primary purpose questions, but the same patterns appear in the other three question types (Specific, Inference, and Function). If you start looking for patterns in how these questions are made difficult, then you will be much more likely to avoid the tricky sucker choice.

Mastering the Common Question Types Summary

Reading Comprehension is a question-driven exercise, much less dependent on true mastery of the passage than people tend to think. Consequently, you should spend a good deal of your study time mastering the four major question types:

- Inference
- Specific
- Function
- Universal

For Inference, Specific, and Function questions, you will almost always need to return to the passage. Your STOP understanding of the passage will point you to the relevant portion of the passage, allowing you to spend your time and energy deconstructing the question and answer choices. With Universal questions, your STOP understanding should almost always point you to the correct answer without needing to re-read any portions of the passage. It is also important that you remember:

- Inference questions will frequently force you to infer. The correct answer is not as often a direct paraphrase of the statement, but requires you to draw a conclusion that is guaranteed by the passage.

- Specific questions are more often asking for nearly verbatim transcriptions from the passage, but be certain to note the specific wording in the question stem. If a question asks for the cause of a reaction, the effect of that reaction makes for a compelling trap answer.

- Overall, pay attention to wordplay and misdirection, and check for context at the paragraph level. Often trap answers look correct from reading a sentence or fragment, but once you have read the sentences around them you will see that they are traps. For example, Function questions can appear to hinge on one sentence ("the governor's plan will never work…"), but the surrounding context will show that the author believes something entirely different ("…if the people do not recognize that it is the only possible solution and that their sacrifice is absolutely vital").

SECTION 4: ADVANCED READING COMPREHENSION SUBJECTS

For most examinees, the natural sciences and overly technical passages prove to be the most difficult. Even those who work in science and technology often struggle to engage with the pure-science topics such as astronomy, botany, and immunology that have been tested on the GMAT, as prior knowledge of these subjects is rare among those who take the GMAT. What makes these topics difficult is often inconsequential to your role as the test-taker. People are often thrown off by:

Technical Language: This even happens in literary passages that invoke academic jargon. Test-takers struggle to pronounce or remember certain words, and in doing so feel their anxiety rise. Remember this: If you don't know a long, technical word, it's probably not a word you need to know, and long words also make for great "bookmarks." As you'll see later in this section, a word like "protoplanetary" or "manifestation" takes up enough horizontal space that it should be relatively easy to find if a question asks about it. And the question will likely hinge on the cause/effect words that surround it, not the definition of that word itself.

Dense Descriptions of Processes and Reactions: People often get lost in the description of a scientific process that they cannot visualize or immediately understand. Remember: Unless the question specifically asks you about particular steps in that process, you may not need to understand it at all. If you cannot conceptualize a scientific description, you can often simply note where it occurs (e.g., "Paragraph two details the antigen-antibody immunological reaction") and go back to dissect it only if a question requires you to do so.

Dry, Explanatory Passages: Some passages, simply put, are "boring," particularly at the end of a long test day when your mind is just ready to turn off. Know, however, that few of your competitors are entranced by their passages, either, so this is not a competitive disadvantage. Build an understanding of the organization of the passages, and then engage yourself with the questions. Your job is not to love or even understand the subject matter, as long as you can answer the questions that accompany the passage.

An Inability to Focus: Long, dense, technical passages have a tendency to make test-takers disengage. Have you ever gotten to the end of the page and realized that you "looked at" but didn't "read" all of the words on the page? Many GMAT passages have this effect, but you have a plan: If you simply cannot focus, build your understanding around structural language and organization, and then come back to content. For example, if one paragraph begins with "Also" and another with "Furthermore," those are likely support paragraphs for a point that came in the first paragraph, and you can build your understanding around that. STOP can be your guide through even the driest, most technical passages.

LESSON

Natural Sciences Passage

Until recently, Ascaris azure, known as the Diaz blueworm, and Ascaris tropica, known as the Costa Rican heatworm, were thought to be different species of roundworm. The heatworm is about 0.5 centimeters long, and lives within the bark of huge cecropia trees in Southeast Asian rain forests. The blueworm, barely visible with the naked eye, is found in frigid seafloors. Despite these apparent differences, the Institute of Helminthological Studies has officially stated that "both" species are actually Diaz blueworms.

Dr. Ginny Bolton, examining roundworm samples collected in Borneo, noticed that the heatworm's tiny cilia (hairlike organelles) appeared to beat in a single direction, aiding in the expulsion of food. Dr. Bolton later determined that the cilia also made it much easier for the heatworm to live in the stifling confines of tree bark. The cilia project from a cuticle that is made of keratin, a protein that protects the worm's epidermis from drying out and overheating. The cilia help regulate the proliferation of the keratin, and the force of the cilia's movements varies as the external temperature changes, allowing for a highly responsive thermostatic system, constantly adjusting the amount of keratin so that the worm would be neither overexposed nor stifled.

Knowing that the only other roundworm with directional cilia is the blueworm, Dr. Bolton consulted with several blueworm specialists. The thermostatic system that served the heatworm so well proved to be identical to the one used by oceangoing blueworm. However, the blueworm, which has been known to colonize methane ice mounds, uses the keratin to protect itself from frigid temperatures. The cilia sensed when the temperature was high enough to allow the production of keratin to slow down. Without the surrounding wall of keratin, the worm can more easily graze on bacteria.

Genetic testing showed that the blueworm and the heatworm were not merely structurally similar; to the scientists' surprise, the worms were identical. This was startling, not only because of their vastly differing habitats, but also because of the difference in size. The answer again was to be found in the keratin, a tough substance that normally inhibits growth, keeping the hydrostatic pressure very high within the worm. The relatively large worm found in the rainforest molts as it grows, allowing the worm to increase its volume a very small amount each time it does, but the smaller worm cannot afford this much exposure. The freezing temperatures trigger the production of keratin so quickly that the worm has little chance to grow, thus keeping its volume approximately one-fourth that of the larger worm.

LEARNING BY DOING
STOP Passage Summary

If you struggled to master the science behind blueworms and heatworms in your first pass through on this passage, you're not alone. Then again, if you truly struggled to do so, you can learn to read more efficiently. When you initially read this passage, the details are unimportant. What is important is the general flow, which you can get from an emphasis on structural language. Ultimately, this passage is organized as follows:

Paragraph one: Introduce blueworms and heatworms, and note that, surprisingly, they're the same species.

Paragraph two: Detail the heatworm (and if you see any specific questions about heatworms, you'll return to this paragraph).

Paragraph three: Detail the blueworm and highlight the reason (directional cilia) that the discovery was possible.

Paragraph four: Compare/contrast the two worms.

Passage Type: Explanatory/descriptive passage with no discernible tone or "angle."

Primary Purpose: To note a fairly surprising discovery, and explain some of the facts behind it.

If you've only gotten this far, you're already ahead of the game. You know specifically where to go for any detail-laden questions (paragraph two if it's about the heatworm; paragraph three if it's about the blueworm; paragraph four if it's a comparative study), and you have a pretty good idea of what the passage is about. It's a fairly surprising discovery that these two seemingly different worms are the same, and the passage goes on to give more details about that discovery.

LESSON

Natural Sciences Passage

Until recently, Ascaris azure, known as the Diaz blueworm, and Ascaris tropica, known as the Costa Rican heatworm, were thought to be different species of roundworm. The heatworm is about 0.5 centimeters long, and lives within the bark of huge cecropia trees in Southeast Asian rain forests. The blueworm, barely visible with the naked eye, is found in frigid seafloors. Despite these apparent differences, the Institute of Helminthological Studies has officially stated that "both" species are actually Diaz blueworms.

Dr. Ginny Bolton, examining roundworm samples collected in Borneo, noticed that the heatworm's tiny cilia (hairlike organelles) appeared to beat in a single direction, aiding in the expulsion of food. Dr. Bolton later determined that the cilia also made it much easier for the heatworm to live in the stifling confines of tree bark. The cilia project from a cuticle that is made of keratin, a protein that protects the worm's epidermis from drying out and overheating. The cilia help regulate the proliferation of the keratin, and the force of the cilia's movements varies as the external temperature changes, allowing for a highly responsive thermostatic system, constantly adjusting the amount of keratin so that the worm would be neither overexposed nor stifled.

Knowing that the only other roundworm with directional cilia is the blueworm, Dr. Bolton consulted with several blueworm specialists. The thermostatic system that served the heatworm so well proved to be identical to the one used by oceangoing blueworm. However, the blueworm, which has been known to colonize methane ice mounds, uses the keratin to protect itself from frigid temperatures. The cilia sensed when the temperature was high enough to allow the production of keratin to slow down. Without the surrounding wall of keratin, the worm can more easily graze on bacteria.

Genetic testing showed that the blueworm and the heatworm were not merely structurally similar; to the scientists' surprise, the worms were identical. This was startling, not only because of their vastly differing habitats, but also because of the difference in size. The answer again was to be found in the keratin, a tough substance that normally inhibits growth, keeping the hydrostatic pressure very high within the worm. The relatively large worm found in the rainforest molts as it grows, allowing the worm to increase its volume a very small amount each time it does, but the smaller worm cannot afford this much exposure. The freezing temperatures trigger the production of keratin so quickly that the worm has little chance to grow, thus keeping its volume approximately one-fourth that of the larger worm.

9.   Which of the following is the primary purpose of the passage?

   (A)   To present an overview of the function of keratin in roundworms

   (B)   To give an example of the kind of discoveries that are still being made in the natural sciences

   (C)   To show the ways in which scientists who are highly specialized need to work together

   (D)   To provide some of the details of a surprising scientific discovery

   (E)   To show how genetic testing is an invaluable scientific tool

LEARNING BY DOING
Scope

Question #9 is a primary purpose question, but essentially it comes down to your analysis of scope. Note that the author never goes above the scope of this particular discovery, so answer choices B, C, and E are unsupported. The author starts with roundworms and ends with details about roundworms; this passage is not an example of any larger agenda. Similarly, answer choice A is too narrow. While keratin does come into play, that's not the main point here. The main point, if you follow the scope of the paragraph-by-paragraph organization above, is to highlight that this is a surprising discovery, and to provide details. That matches just about verbatim with answer choice D, the correct answer. Extrapolating this to future questions, recognize that a good understanding of scope—without any real need to understand any of the scientific details—is sufficient to answer this question correctly.

THINK LIKE THE TESTMAKER
Hiding the Right Answer and Selling the Wrong Answer

The "trap" answers on this question, particularly answer choices B and C, may be tempting primarily because they take this essay in a direction that you may want it to go. As an aspiring captain of industry, you likely don't care much about roundworms, but as a manager you would like to campaign for more collaboration across research and development departments or for a higher R&D budget. The trap answers here add context that your mind would like to have, but that doesn't exist in the passage itself.

In this way, primary purpose questions act a bit like Inference questions: The correct answer must be true, but it need not be "compelling" or "exciting."

Natural Sciences Passage

Until recently, Ascaris azure, known as the Diaz blueworm, and Ascaris tropica, known as the Costa Rican heatworm, were thought to be different species of roundworm. The heatworm is about 0.5 centimeters long, and lives within the bark of huge cecropia trees in Southeast Asian rain forests. The blueworm, barely visible with the naked eye, is found in frigid seafloors. Despite these apparent differences, the Institute of Helminthological Studies has officially stated that "both" species are actually Diaz blueworms.

Dr. Ginny Bolton, examining roundworm samples collected in Borneo, noticed that the heatworm's tiny cilia (hairlike organelles) appeared to beat in a single direction, aiding in the expulsion of food. Dr. Bolton later determined that the cilia also made it much easier for the heatworm to live in the stifling confines of tree bark. The cilia project from a cuticle that is made of keratin, a protein that protects the worm's epidermis from drying out and overheating. The cilia help regulate the proliferation of the keratin, and the force of the cilia's movements varies as the external temperature changes, allowing for a highly responsive thermostatic system, constantly adjusting the amount of keratin so that the worm would be neither overexposed nor stifled.

Knowing that the only other roundworm with directional cilia is the blueworm, Dr. Bolton consulted with several blueworm specialists. The thermostatic system that served the heatworm so well proved to be identical to the one used by oceangoing blueworm. However, the blueworm, which has been known to colonize methane ice mounds, uses the keratin to protect itself from frigid temperatures. The cilia sensed when the temperature was high enough to allow the production of keratin to slow down. Without the surrounding wall of keratin, the worm can more easily graze on bacteria.

Genetic testing showed that the blueworm and the heatworm were not merely structurally similar; to the scientists' surprise, the worms were identical. This was startling, not only because of their vastly differing habitats, but also because of the difference in size. The answer again was to be found in the keratin, a tough substance that normally inhibits growth, keeping the hydrostatic pressure very high within the worm. The relatively large worm found in the rainforest molts as it grows, allowing the worm to increase its volume a very small amount each time it does, but the smaller worm cannot afford this much exposure. The freezing temperatures trigger the production of keratin so quickly that the worm has little chance to grow, thus keeping its volume approximately one-fourth that of the larger worm.

10. According to the passage, in what way do the blueworm's cilia aid the worm in coping with extreme heat and cold?

    (A) They help with the removal of food from the worm's system.

    (B) They provide a mechanism by which the production of keratin can be regulated.

    (C) They collect the bacteria on which some blueworms graze.

    (D) They keep the hydrostatic pressure within the worm high.

    (E) They keep it securely attached to the bark of the cecropia tree.

LESSON

LEARNING BY DOING
Organization and Cause/Effect

To answer question #10, your main objective is simply to follow the organization of the passage. The question asks specifically about the blueworm, so you should know to look in paragraph three. And the question specifically asks about the role of cilia with regard to heat and cold, so from there you need to follow the cause/effect relationships. The fourth sentence says, specifically, "the cilia sensed when the temperature was high enough to allow the production of keratin to slow down." This sentence should lead you directly to answer choice B, the correct answer. The cilia sense temperature in order to slow down the production of keratin.

SKILLS MEET STRATEGY
Specific Detail and Organization

What makes this question difficult? For many students, it is simply the time that it takes to locate the relevant few sentences and to process the scientific data within them. For other students, that creates the difficulty in the passage as a whole: Reading about these worms, their cilia, keratin production, etc. takes some time and attention to detail to process. Once you first know where to locate the information, and second process that direct cause-and-effect relationship, the question itself is fairly straightforward. The degree of difficulty here is really just the opportunity for you to waste large chunks of time, making the rest of the Verbal section that much tougher to complete successfully.

This is why it is so important to read for organization first, and to avoid becoming mired in details in your initial read. Even if you had spent four to five minutes reading this passage at first, you would have to have returned to the passage to double-check that particular relationship, so that extra up-front time would not have proved to be well spent. And if you didn't have a good grasp of the organization (blueworm = paragraph three), you'd have wasted time searching key words to answer the question. Reading for organization and primary purpose sets you up to succeed efficiently on later questions.

LESSON

Natural Sciences Passage

Until recently, Ascaris azure, known as the Diaz blueworm, and Ascaris tropica, known as the Costa Rican heatworm, were thought to be different species of roundworm. The heatworm is about 0.5 centimeters long, and lives within the bark of huge cecropia trees in Southeast Asian rain forests. The blueworm, barely visible with the naked eye, is found in frigid seafloors. Despite these apparent differences, the Institute of Helminthological Studies has officially stated that "both" species are actually Diaz blueworms.

Dr. Ginny Bolton, examining roundworm samples collected in Borneo, noticed that the heatworm's tiny cilia (hairlike organelles) appeared to beat in a single direction, aiding in the expulsion of food. Dr. Bolton later determined that the cilia also made it much easier for the heatworm to live in the stifling confines of tree bark. The cilia project from a cuticle that is made of keratin, a protein that protects the worm's epidermis from drying out and overheating. The cilia help regulate the proliferation of the keratin, and the force of the cilia's movements varies as the external temperature changes, allowing for a highly responsive thermostatic system, constantly adjusting the amount of keratin so that the worm would be neither overexposed nor stifled.

Knowing that the only other roundworm with directional cilia is the blueworm, Dr. Bolton consulted with several blueworm specialists. The thermostatic system that served the heatworm so well proved to be identical to the one used by oceangoing blueworm. However, the blueworm, which has been known to colonize methane ice mounds, uses the keratin to protect itself from frigid temperatures. The cilia sensed when the temperature was high enough to allow the production of keratin to slow down. Without the surrounding wall of keratin, the worm can more easily graze on bacteria.

Genetic testing showed that the blueworm and the heatworm were not merely structurally similar; to the scientists' surprise, the worms were identical. This was startling, not only because of their vastly differing habitats, but also because of the difference in size. The answer again was to be found in the keratin, a tough substance that normally inhibits growth, keeping the hydrostatic pressure very high within the worm. The relatively large worm found in the rainforest molts as it grows, allowing the worm to increase its volume a very small amount each time it does, but the smaller worm cannot afford this much exposure. The freezing temperatures trigger the production of keratin so quickly that the worm has little chance to grow, thus keeping its volume approximately one-fourth that of the larger worm.

11. It can be inferred from the passage that, compared to blueworms found in the sea, heatworms found in rainforests _____.

    (A) do not graze on bacteria

    (B) do not have high levels of hydrostatic pressure

    (C) cannot survive in water

    (D) have little chance to grow because of extreme temperature

    (E) replace keratin more slowly

LESSON

LEARNING BY DOING
Inferences Require You to Leverage Information

With question #11, you should know up front that the answer will be found in the final paragraph, based on the organization notes above that paragraph four is the "compare/contrast" paragraph. From there, however, look how the authors hide the correct answer, answer choice E. The question asks about heatworms, but the operative sentence in the last paragraph is about blueworms: "The freezing temperature trigger the production of keratin so quickly that the (smaller) worm has little chance to grow...." The passage explicitly states that the blueworm produces keratin much more quickly than does the heatworm. This leads, via an inference, to answer choice E: It must be true that the heatworm, then, produces keratin much more slowly.

On these Inference questions (this one began "It can be inferred from the passage..."), you should be prepared to infer, not just to regurgitate. The authors of these passages know that you're apt to be intimidated by technical information, but know also that you don't need to be able to understand much about these worms to have drawn that inference. If one is faster, the other by definition is slower. When the question says "infer," be prepared to leverage the given information into what is often a fairly natural second piece of information (if A > B, then B < A).

LESSON

Natural Sciences Passage

Until recently, Ascaris azure, known as the Diaz blueworm, and Ascaris tropica, known as the Costa Rican heatworm, were thought to be different species of roundworm. The heatworm is about 0.5 centimeters long, and lives within the bark of huge cecropia trees in Southeast Asian rain forests. The blueworm, barely visible with the naked eye, is found in frigid seafloors. Despite these apparent differences, the Institute of Helminthological Studies has officially stated that "both" species are actually Diaz blueworms.

Dr. Ginny Bolton, examining roundworm samples collected in Borneo, noticed that the heatworm's tiny cilia (hairlike organelles) appeared to beat in a single direction, aiding in the expulsion of food. Dr. Bolton later determined that the cilia also made it much easier for the heatworm to live in the stifling confines of tree bark. The cilia project from a cuticle that is made of keratin, a protein that protects the worm's epidermis from drying out and overheating. The cilia help regulate the proliferation of the keratin, and the force of the cilia's movements varies as the external temperature changes, allowing for a highly responsive thermostatic system, constantly adjusting the amount of keratin so that the worm would be neither overexposed nor stifled.

Knowing that the only other roundworm with directional cilia is the blueworm, Dr. Bolton consulted with several blueworm specialists. The thermostatic system that served the heatworm so well proved to be identical to the one used by oceangoing blueworm. However, the blueworm, which has been known to colonize methane ice mounds, uses the keratin to protect itself from frigid temperatures. The cilia sensed when the temperature was high enough to allow the production of keratin to slow down. Without the surrounding wall of keratin, the worm can more easily graze on bacteria.

Genetic testing showed that the blueworm and the heatworm were not merely structurally similar; to the scientists' surprise, the worms were identical. This was startling, not only because of their vastly differing habitats, but also because of the difference in size. The answer again was to be found in the keratin, a tough substance that normally inhibits growth, keeping the hydrostatic pressure very high within the worm. The relatively large worm found in the rainforest molts as it grows, allowing the worm to increase its volume a very small amount each time it does, but the smaller worm cannot afford this much exposure. The freezing temperatures trigger the production of keratin so quickly that the worm has little chance to grow, thus keeping its volume approximately one-fourth that of the larger worm.

12. It can be inferred from the passage that if the cilia of a blueworm found on the seafloor were to become damaged, preventing the sensing of warmer temperatures, the worm _____.

(A) could grow to a length of 0.5 centimeters

(B) would be in danger of freezing

(C) might not be able to gain access to enough nourishment to sustain life

(D) would be forced to find its way to warmer temperatures

(E) would experience a sudden drop of hydrostatic pressure

LESSON

LEARNING BY DOING
Organization and Inference

Question #12 is quite similar to the earlier question about blueworms, and you should already know to head directly to paragraph three for that specific information. In that earlier question, we determined that the role of cilia was to sense warmer temperatures and control the production of keratin. Again, your job is to follow cause-and-effect relationships and, when the question asks you to "infer," to recognize that you will likely have to leverage information. Here the next step is that "without the wall of keratin, the worm can more easily graze on bacteria." This means that the cause/effect flowchart would read: cilia → sense temperature → slow production of keratin → allow worm to eat. This means that without the cilia, the effects that follow would also not occur. Therefore, answer choice C is correct: Without the properly functioning cilia, the worm might not be able to obtain enough nourishment.

Natural Sciences Passage

Until recently, Ascaris azure, known as the Diaz blueworm, and Ascaris tropica, known as the Costa Rican heatworm, were thought to be different species of roundworm. The heatworm is about 0.5 centimeters long, and lives within the bark of huge cecropia trees in Southeast Asian rain forests. The blueworm, barely visible with the naked eye, is found in frigid seafloors. Despite these apparent differences, the Institute of Helminthological Studies has officially stated that "both" species are actually Diaz blueworms.

Dr. Ginny Bolton, examining roundworm samples collected in Borneo, noticed that the heatworm's tiny cilia (hairlike organelles) appeared to beat in a single direction, aiding in the expulsion of food. Dr. Bolton later determined that the cilia also made it much easier for the heatworm to live in the stifling confines of tree bark. The cilia project from a cuticle that is made of keratin, a protein that protects the worm's epidermis from drying out and overheating. The cilia help regulate the proliferation of the keratin, and the force of the cilia's movements varies as the external temperature changes, allowing for a highly responsive thermostatic system, constantly adjusting the amount of keratin so that the worm would be neither overexposed nor stifled.

Knowing that the only other roundworm with directional cilia is the blueworm, Dr. Bolton consulted with several blueworm specialists. The thermostatic system that served the heatworm so well proved to be identical to the one used by oceangoing blueworm. However, the blueworm, which has been known to colonize methane ice mounds, uses the keratin to protect itself from frigid temperatures. The cilia sensed when the temperature was high enough to allow the production of keratin to slow down. Without the surrounding wall of keratin, the worm can more easily graze on bacteria.

Genetic testing showed that the blueworm and the heatworm were not merely structurally similar; to the scientists' surprise, the worms were identical. This was startling, not only because of their vastly differing habitats, but also because of the difference in size. The answer again was to be found in the keratin, a tough substance that normally inhibits growth, keeping the hydrostatic pressure very high within the worm. The relatively large worm found in the rainforest molts as it grows, allowing the worm to increase its volume a very small amount each time it does, but the smaller worm cannot afford this much exposure. The freezing temperatures trigger the production of keratin so quickly that the worm has little chance to grow, thus keeping its volume approximately one-fourth that of the larger worm.

13. According to the passage, researchers were able to make the discovery of the unlikely relationship between the two worms because of which of the following?

    (A) Both worms have mechanisms to produce keratin.

    (B) Both worms exist in extreme temperatures.

    (C) Both worms are researched by the Institute of Helminthological Studies.

    (D) Both worms feature directional cilia.

    (E) Both worms molt as they grow.

LESSON

LEARNING BY DOING
Follow the Theory

If you have properly read for organization, question #13 should be quite manageable. Paragraph three starts with the answer: Dr. Bolton was able to make the discovery because both worms have directional cilia. Therefore, answer choice D is correct.

More strategically, remember this about natural science passages: In your initial read, you are not responsible for any scientific details, but you will often need to "follow the theory"—as long as you know what happens to the theory. (Was it confirmed? Overruled? How was it discovered?) If you make a special note, as you should have here, about the general flow of "the theory," then you will be rewarded. You will usually need to go back to re-read any intense details, anyway, so focus your initial read on organization.

THINK LIKE THE TESTMAKER
The Rewards System

To summarize the passage and its questions, look at what you've answered: a primary purpose question; a Specific detail, cause/effect question; two Inference questions; and a question about "following the theory." For an aspiring MBA student, this makes sense. The authors of the GMAT are assessing whether you can quickly identify if/then, cause/ effect relationships; whether you can sift through technical data (you'll outsource that to the egghead scientists when you're a manager) to find the cruxes of the argument; and whether you can glean the author's true intent. That is why the "follow the theory" mentality is apt to help you when you see scientific, technical passages: The GMAT cannot be about your scientific acumen, but is rather about your ability to derive a "managerial understanding" or executive summary of the reasons behind a theory or conclusion. The science is often the smokescreen; most natural science passages are about the pure sciences and not the applied sciences, mainly so that few if any test-takers will have thorough understanding of the subject matter and therefore so everyone will need to read strategically. Knowing this, you can adjust the way you read away from details and toward organization, and be rewarded for that when you reach the questions.

LESSON

Technical Passage

While popular science tends to favor extragalactic astronomical research that emphasizes current challenges to physics, such as the existence of dark matter, dark energy, and Cosmic inflation, significant research continues to take place in the field of planetary astronomy on the formation of our own solar system. In early attempts to explain this phenomenon, astronomers believed in the encounter, or "rogue star," hypothesis, which suggests that matter was tidally stripped away from our sun as a larger star passed within a gravitationally significant distance some billions of years ago. The encounter hypothesis postulates that after being stripped away, the matter cooled as it spun farther from the sun, and formed planets with their own centers of gravity. This hypothesis conveniently accounts for the fact that all planets in the solar system revolve in the same direction around the sun; it is also consistent with the denser planets remaining closer to the sun, and the more gaseous planets traveling further away.

The encounter hypothesis explained the phenomenon sufficiently enough that it allowed scientists to focus on more immediately rewarding topics in physics and astronomy for most of the first half of the 20th century. Closer investigation, however, found several significant problems with the encounter hypothesis, most notably that the hot gas pulled from the sun would not condense to form dense planets, but rather would expand in the absence of a central, gravitational force. Furthermore, the statistical unlikelihood of a star passing in the (astronomically speaking) short time of the sun's existence required scientists to abandon the encounter hypothesis in search of a new explanation. Soon after, astronomers formed a second theory, the nebular hypothesis, which submits that the solar system began as a large cloud of gas containing the matter that would form the sun and its orbiting planets. The nebular hypothesis suggests that when the cloud reached a critical mass, it collapsed under its own gravity. The resulting angular momentum would have morphed the nebula into a protoplanetary disc, with a dense center that generated intense heat and pressure, and a cooler, thinner mass that revolved around it. The central mass would have continued to build in density and heat, forming the sun, while the centrifugal force around the disc's edge kept smaller masses from being pulled in to the sun; those masses, upon cooling, would break off to become planets held in orbit by the competing gravitational force of the sun and centrifugal force of their orbital inertia.

The nebular hypothesis, however well it explained the sun's formation, remained problematic in its ability to account for the formation of several planets with differing physical and chemical properties. Encouraged by their advance toward a provable hypothesis for the solar system, scientists have recently come to adopt a third hypothesis, the protoplanet hypothesis. This currently accepted theory holds that the

gaseous cloud that would form the solar system was composed of particles so cold that even the heat of the forming sun could not significantly impact the temperature of the outer reaches of the cloud. Gas in the inner region, within what scientists refer to as the frost line, was quickly either burned or dispersed, leaving a small amount of metallic matter, such as nickel and iron, to form the inner planets. Such matter would need to have an extremely high melting point to avoid becoming liquefied, ensuring that Mercury, Venus, Earth, and Mars would remain small and dense. Outside the frost line, however, gas was kept cool enough to remain in solid, icy states. Over time, planets such as Jupiter and Saturn would amass large quantities of frozen gas, enough to grow to hundreds of times the size of the Earth.

LESSON

LEARNING BY DOING
Structural Language Is Your Guide

This passage is dense with terminology, but your mantra on a highly technical passage should be to focus on the words you know, and don't worry as much about those you don't. While this passage is littered with technical language, the true flow of the theory hinges on transitional language. The first paragraph introduces the encounter hypothesis, and then in the second paragraph you should be drawn to the word "however" in the second sentence. That transition sets up "significant problems" with the initial theory, and the word "furthermore" in the next sentence expands on those problems. If you're following the theory, then you should recognize right afterward that "astronomers formed a second theory," and that gives you the primary purpose of the second paragraph: to show the problems with the first theory and how those problems led to the formation of a second theory. By following the transitional language and paying attention to numerical terms (note that "a third hypothesis" is the theme of the last paragraph), you can find the organization of this passage:

Paragraph one: Introduce the encounter hypothesis for the formation of the solar system

Paragraph two: Discuss problems with that theory, and introduce a second (the nebular hypothesis)

Paragraph three: Discuss limitations with the second theory, and introduce a third (the protoplanet hypothesis)

Passage Type: Explanatory/descriptive passage

Primary Purpose: The purpose of the passage is to describe the evolution of three theories of the formation of the solar system.

From this outline, you should know where to go for Specific questions, and you can glean the primary purpose: to explain the evolution of (three) theories of the formation of the solar system. At this point, you are set up for success on the questions that follow.

Technical Passage

While popular science tends to favor extragalactic astronomical research that emphasizes current challenges to physics, such as the existence of dark matter, dark energy, and Cosmic inflation, significant research continues to take place in the field of planetary astronomy on the formation of our own solar system. In early attempts to explain this phenomenon, astronomers believed in the encounter, or "rogue star," hypothesis, which suggests that matter was tidally stripped away from our sun as a larger star passed within a gravitationally significant distance some billions of years ago. The encounter hypothesis postulates that after being stripped away, the matter cooled as it spun farther from the sun, and formed planets with their own centers of gravity. This hypothesis conveniently accounts for the fact that all planets in the solar system revolve in the same direction around the sun; it is also consistent with the denser planets remaining closer to the sun, and the more gaseous planets traveling further away.

The encounter hypothesis explained the phenomenon sufficiently enough that it allowed scientists to focus on more immediately rewarding topics in physics and astronomy for most of the first half of the 20th century. Closer investigation, however, found several significant problems with the encounter hypothesis, most notably that the hot gas pulled from the sun would not condense to form dense planets, but rather would expand in the absence of a central, gravitational force. Furthermore, the statistical unlikelihood of a star passing in the (astronomically speaking) short time of the sun's existence required scientists to abandon the encounter hypothesis in search of a new explanation. Soon after, astronomers formed a second theory, the nebular hypothesis, which submits that the solar system began as a large cloud of gas containing the matter that would form the sun and its orbiting planets. The nebular hypothesis suggests that when the cloud reached a critical mass, it collapsed under its own gravity. The resulting angular momentum would have morphed the nebula into a protoplanetary disc, with a dense center that generated intense heat and pressure, and a cooler, thinner mass that revolved around it. The central mass would have continued to build in density and heat, forming the sun, while the centrifugal force around the disc's edge kept smaller masses from being pulled in to the sun; those masses, upon cooling, would break off to become planets held in orbit by the competing gravitational force of the sun and centrifugal force of their orbital inertia.

The nebular hypothesis, however well it explained the sun's formation, remained problematic in its ability to account for the formation of several planets with differing physical and chemical properties. Encouraged by their advance toward a provable hypothesis for the solar system, scientists have recently come to adopt a third hypothesis, the protoplanet hypothesis. This currently accepted theory holds that the

gaseous cloud that would form the solar system was composed of particles so cold that even the heat of the forming sun could not significantly impact the temperature of the outer reaches of the cloud. Gas in the inner region, within what scientists refer to as the frost line, was quickly either burned or dispersed, leaving a small amount of metallic matter, such as nickel and iron, to form the inner planets. Such matter would need to have an extremely high melting point to avoid becoming liquefied, ensuring that Mercury, Venus, Earth, and Mars would remain small and dense. Outside the frost line, however, gas was kept cool enough to remain in solid, icy states. Over time, planets such as Jupiter and Saturn would amass large quantities of frozen gas, enough to grow to hundreds of times the size of the Earth.

14. The passage is primarily concerned with which of the following?

   (A) Describing the manner in which our sun was formed from gaseous material

   (B) Criticizing the encounter hypothesis and its explanation of the formation of the solar system

   (C) Explaining three theories for the formation of our solar system

   (D) Proving that the planets of the solar system have similar compositions

   (E) Detailing a research study regarding the origins of the solar system

LEARNING BY DOING
Primary Purpose

Question #14 is a standard primary purpose question. Remember: The most common way that people miss these questions is to pick an answer choice that is too narrow in scope. If you have correctly identified the purposes of each paragraph, as above, you should know that answer choice B, a popular trap answer, is only one of three paragraphs (the second), and is therefore far too narrow. The correct answer choice, C, is bland but covers well the flow of the entire essay. Beware the primary purpose answer choice that is a major portion of one or two paragraphs, but that does not capture the entire passage.

SKILLS MEET STRATEGY
Tone and Primary Purpose

Notice the first words of some of the answer choices: "criticizing" and "proving," most notably, in answer choices B and D, respectively. Neither is consistent with the author's explanatory tone. In the same way that the first words of bullets on your MBA application resume matter, the active verbs beginning answer choices in Reading Comprehension are as important (if not more) as what follows. If the actions seem too strong or out of touch with the author's tone, you have a good reason to eliminate (or at least call into serious question) those choices immediately.

LESSON

Technical Passage

While popular science tends to favor extragalactic astronomical research that emphasizes current challenges to physics, such as the existence of dark matter, dark energy, and Cosmic inflation, significant research continues to take place in the field of planetary astronomy on the formation of our own solar system. In early attempts to explain this phenomenon, astronomers believed in the encounter, or "rogue star," hypothesis, which suggests that matter was tidally stripped away from our sun as a larger star passed within a gravitationally significant distance some billions of years ago. The encounter hypothesis postulates that after being stripped away, the matter cooled as it spun farther from the sun, and formed planets with their own centers of gravity. This hypothesis conveniently accounts for the fact that all planets in the solar system revolve in the same direction around the sun; it is also consistent with the denser planets remaining closer to the sun, and the more gaseous planets traveling further away.

The encounter hypothesis explained the phenomenon sufficiently enough that it allowed scientists to focus on more immediately rewarding topics in physics and astronomy for most of the first half of the 20th century. Closer investigation, however, found several significant problems with the encounter hypothesis, most notably that the hot gas pulled from the sun would not condense to form dense planets, but rather would expand in the absence of a central, gravitational force. Furthermore, the statistical unlikelihood of a star passing in the (astronomically speaking) short time of the sun's existence required scientists to abandon the encounter hypothesis in search of a new explanation. Soon after, astronomers formed a second theory, the nebular hypothesis, which submits that the solar system began as a large cloud of gas containing the matter that would form the sun and its orbiting planets. The nebular hypothesis suggests that when the cloud reached a critical mass, it collapsed under its own gravity. The resulting angular momentum would have morphed the nebula into a protoplanetary disc, with a dense center that generated intense heat and pressure, and a cooler, thinner mass that revolved around it. The central mass would have continued to build in density and heat, forming the sun, while the centrifugal force around the disc's edge kept smaller masses from being pulled in to the sun; those masses, upon cooling, would break off to become planets held in orbit by the competing gravitational force of the sun and centrifugal force of their orbital inertia.

The nebular hypothesis, however well it explained the sun's formation, remained problematic in its ability to account for the formation of several planets with differing physical and chemical properties. Encouraged by their advance toward a provable hypothesis for the solar system, scientists have recently come to adopt a third hypothesis, the protoplanet hypothesis. This currently accepted theory holds that the

gaseous cloud that would form the solar system was composed of particles so cold that even the heat of the forming sun could not significantly impact the temperature of the outer reaches of the cloud. Gas in the inner region, within what scientists refer to as the frost line, was quickly either burned or dispersed, leaving a small amount of metallic matter, such as nickel and iron, to form the inner planets. Such matter would need to have an extremely high melting point to avoid becoming liquefied, ensuring that Mercury, Venus, Earth, and Mars would remain small and dense. Outside the frost line, however, gas was kept cool enough to remain in solid, icy states. Over time, planets such as Jupiter and Saturn would amass large quantities of frozen gas, enough to grow to hundreds of times the size of the Earth.

15. According to the nebular hypothesis, a protoplanetary disc formed in the early stages of the solar system because _____.

   (A) cold gases in the outer reaches of the nebula were repelled from the hot center of the spiraling mass

   (B) gravity forced the nebular cloud to contract upon itself, creating significant angular momentum

   (C) cooling matter held safely from the center of the mass could eventually form planets

   (D) matter with a high melting point could not be consumed by the heat in the center of the disc

   (E) gravity from a passing star pulled matter away from the sun, allowing planets to form around it

LEARNING BY DOING
Cause and Effect

Question #15 is a classic natural sciences cause-and-effect, Specific detail question. The key to these questions is to pay particular attention to what the question asks for, because in most of these questions both the cause and effect will be answer choices—one the bait, and the other correct. Here, the question asks for the cause of the protoplanetary disc, so you can rest assured that one trap answer will be something that results from that disc.

The question stem itself gives you a large clue: Even if you didn't grasp enough of the details to know specifically where the protoplanetary disc was discussed, the stem points you to the nebular hypothesis, meaning that you should look in paragraph two. There, you will find this description: "…when the cloud reached a critical mass, it collapsed under its own gravity. The resulting angular momentum would have morphed the nebula into a protoplanetary disc…." So the cause is the angular momentum for the gravitational collapse, matching exactly with answer choice B. Answer choice C is an effect of the protoplanetary disc, so be careful of just performing a word search and finding correlated terms. When a question asks for a cause or an effect, spend an extra second confirming which you are tasked with finding.

Technical Passage

While popular science tends to favor extragalactic astronomical research that emphasizes current challenges to physics, such as the existence of dark matter, dark energy, and Cosmic inflation, significant research continues to take place in the field of planetary astronomy on the formation of our own solar system. In early attempts to explain this phenomenon, astronomers believed in the encounter, or "rogue star," hypothesis, which suggests that matter was tidally stripped away from our sun as a larger star passed within a gravitationally significant distance some billions of years ago. The encounter hypothesis postulates that after being stripped away, the matter cooled as it spun farther from the sun, and formed planets with their own centers of gravity. This hypothesis conveniently accounts for the fact that all planets in the solar system revolve in the same direction around the sun; it is also consistent with the denser planets remaining closer to the sun, and the more gaseous planets traveling further away.

The encounter hypothesis explained the phenomenon sufficiently enough that it allowed scientists to focus on more immediately rewarding topics in physics and astronomy for most of the first half of the 20th century. Closer investigation, however, found several significant problems with the encounter hypothesis, most notably that the hot gas pulled from the sun would not condense to form dense planets, but rather would expand in the absence of a central, gravitational force. Furthermore, the statistical unlikelihood of a star passing in the (astronomically speaking) short time of the sun's existence required scientists to abandon the encounter hypothesis in search of a new explanation. Soon after, astronomers formed a second theory, the nebular hypothesis, which submits that the solar system began as a large cloud of gas containing the matter that would form the sun and its orbiting planets. The nebular hypothesis suggests that when the cloud reached a critical mass, it collapsed under its own gravity. The resulting angular momentum would have morphed the nebula into a protoplanetary disc, with a dense center that generated intense heat and pressure, and a cooler, thinner mass that revolved around it. The central mass would have continued to build in density and heat, forming the sun, while the centrifugal force around the disc's edge kept smaller masses from being pulled in to the sun; those masses, upon cooling, would break off to become planets held in orbit by the competing gravitational force of the sun and centrifugal force of their orbital inertia.

The nebular hypothesis, however well it explained the sun's formation, remained problematic in its ability to account for the formation of several planets with differing physical and chemical properties. Encouraged by their advance toward a provable hypothesis for the solar system, scientists have recently come to adopt a third hypothesis, the protoplanet hypothesis. This currently accepted theory holds that the

gaseous cloud that would form the solar system was composed of particles so cold that even the heat of the forming sun could not significantly impact the temperature of the outer reaches of the cloud. Gas in the inner region, within what scientists refer to as the frost line, was quickly either burned or dispersed, leaving a small amount of metallic matter, such as nickel and iron, to form the inner planets. Such matter would need to have an extremely high melting point to avoid becoming liquefied, ensuring that Mercury, Venus, Earth, and Mars would remain small and dense. Outside the frost line, however, gas was kept cool enough to remain in solid, icy states. Over time, planets such as Jupiter and Saturn would amass large quantities of frozen gas, enough to grow to hundreds of times the size of the Earth.

16. Which of the following discoveries, if true, would best support the protoplanet hypothesis that the temperature difference is responsible for the different sizes of planets on either side of the frost line?

   (A) The core of Saturn and the core of Mercury are found to be 98% composed of the same materials.

   (B) The cores of Saturn and Jupiter are found to each contain at least five chemical elements not found in the other.

   (C) The core of the Earth and the core of Mars are found to be comprised of the same mix of chemical elements.

   (D) A nearby star is found to be orbited by six planets, and the size of each is inversely proportional to its distance from the star.

   (E) The Earth's moon is found to have a vastly different composition from that of the moons of Jupiter.

LESSON

LEARNING BY DOING
Critical Reasoning in Reading Comprehension

While they do not occur frequently, some Critical Reasoning question formats do appear in Reading Comprehension, and question #16 is a prime example. When this does come up, the portion of the passage referred by the question stem takes the role of the stimulus, and you will provide new information that either strengthens or weakens the conclusion drawn by that segment.

Here, the "conclusion" is part of the protoplanet hypothesis, which is discussed in paragraph three, so you'll want to return there for context. The portion that pertains to temperature difference suggests that the inner planets would be composed of dense elements with high melting points, and the outer planets would be composed of more gaseous elements. To strengthen that hypothesis, then, the correct answer should be consistent with "planets close to the sun are similar to one another, and planets far from the sun are close to one another." Answer choice C, the correct answer, provides evidence along those lines: If Earth and Mars, adjacent planets on the same side of the "frost line," are composed of the same mix of elements, that is consistent with that portion of the theory. Note that other answer choices, such as answer choice A, posit that planets far from each other are similar; this conflicts with the theory and would weaken that hypothesis.

SKILLS MEET STRATEGY
The GMAT Is Integrated

This question can also demonstrate something to you about the way that you study the GMAT. Reading Comprehension involves quite a bit of Critical Reasoning, just as Problem Solving questions often involve elements of Reading Comprehension. (Read carefully!) While the GMAT has one section labeled "Integrated Reasoning," most of the test is actually quite integrated, even if it's not labeled that way. Use practice questions of all varieties to sharpen your reasoning and critical reading skills. For Reading Comprehension specifically, your initiative to pay attention to key structural words will pay dividends as you approach Critical Reasoning and Integrated Reasoning questions and as you write your AWA essay.

LESSON

Technical Passage

While popular science tends to favor extragalactic astronomical research that emphasizes current challenges to physics, such as the existence of dark matter, dark energy, and Cosmic inflation, significant research continues to take place in the field of planetary astronomy on the formation of our own solar system. In early attempts to explain this phenomenon, astronomers believed in the encounter, or "rogue star," hypothesis, which suggests that matter was tidally stripped away from our sun as a larger star passed within a gravitationally significant distance some billions of years ago. The encounter hypothesis postulates that after being stripped away, the matter cooled as it spun farther from the sun, and formed planets with their own centers of gravity. This hypothesis conveniently accounts for the fact that all planets in the solar system revolve in the same direction around the sun; it is also consistent with the denser planets remaining closer to the sun, and the more gaseous planets traveling further away.

The encounter hypothesis explained the phenomenon sufficiently enough that it allowed scientists to focus on more immediately rewarding topics in physics and astronomy for most of the first half of the 20th century. Closer investigation, however, found several significant problems with the encounter hypothesis, most notably that the hot gas pulled from the sun would not condense to form dense planets, but rather would expand in the absence of a central, gravitational force. Furthermore, the statistical unlikelihood of a star passing in the (astronomically speaking) short time of the sun's existence required scientists to abandon the encounter hypothesis in search of a new explanation. Soon after, astronomers formed a second theory, the nebular hypothesis, which submits that the solar system began as a large cloud of gas containing the matter that would form the sun and its orbiting planets. The nebular hypothesis suggests that when the cloud reached a critical mass, it collapsed under its own gravity. The resulting angular momentum would have morphed the nebula into a protoplanetary disc, with a dense center that generated intense heat and pressure, and a cooler, thinner mass that revolved around it. The central mass would have continued to build in density and heat, forming the sun, while the centrifugal force around the disc's edge kept smaller masses from being pulled in to the sun; those masses, upon cooling, would break off to become planets held in orbit by the competing gravitational force of the sun and centrifugal force of their orbital inertia.

The nebular hypothesis, however well it explained the sun's formation, remained problematic in its ability to account for the formation of several planets with differing physical and chemical properties. Encouraged by their advance toward a provable hypothesis for the solar system, scientists have recently come to adopt a third hypothesis, the protoplanet hypothesis. This currently accepted theory holds that the

gaseous cloud that would form the solar system was composed of particles so cold that even the heat of the forming sun could not significantly impact the temperature of the outer reaches of the cloud. Gas in the inner region, within what scientists refer to as the frost line, was quickly either burned or dispersed, leaving a small amount of metallic matter, such as nickel and iron, to form the inner planets. Such matter would need to have an extremely high melting point to avoid becoming liquefied, ensuring that Mercury, Venus, Earth, and Mars would remain small and dense. Outside the frost line, however, gas was kept cool enough to remain in solid, icy states. Over time, planets such as Jupiter and Saturn would amass large quantities of frozen gas, enough to grow to hundreds of times the size of the Earth.

17. The author most likely believes that the nebular hypothesis _____.

   (A) is incorrect

   (B) was accepted without adequate research

   (C) is a partial explanation

   (D) is the most complete of the three hypotheses

   (E) does not properly explain the presence of a "rogue star"

LESSON

LEARNING BY DOING
The Author's Intent

When questions, such as #17, ask you about the author's beliefs, scope, and tone should be your guides. This passage is written in an explanatory fashion, describing the evolution of these theories; the author does not make any emphatic statements about correctness or incorrectness, but rather describes the history of these hypotheses. So answer choices A and B should be held to a higher standard; it's unlikely that the author would have such a universal opinion. If you follow the scope of the nebular hypothesis (the second, found primarily in paragraph two, with qualifiers in paragraph three), you'll see that the author only finds a few limitations to that theory, and that those limitations are researched in paragraph three with the protoplanet hypothesis. Accordingly, you can see that the author feels that the nebular hypothesis is partially correct, but needed more research. Essentially, this leads to correct answer choice C.

Advanced Reading Comprehension Subjects Summary

Technical passages create a challenge for many test-takers, but by this point in the lesson you should recognize that their bark is often much louder than their bite. If you read for STOP and see the dense, technical subject matter for what it is—often just a smokescreen to distract you from your mission—you can consider these passages your competitive advantage. To do so, remember the following:

- Focus on the words you know, not on those you don't. If a term is overly technical, hard to pronounce, or just confusing, it's probably only a term that you need to recognize, not one that you need to understand. But if a term signals organization or structure, that's a word you should give your full attention.

- Read for purpose and organization, not for detail. In a dense passage with dozens of details, you will still only see a handful of questions. Most of those details will not matter, so do not try to understand them all in one read of the passage. Instead, try to understand the author's intent and structure, which will point you to where you need to go to learn about the two or three details that do come up in the questions.

- Follow the theory. Most technical passages are structured so that the details support the author's narration of a scientific discovery or history. If you can follow what happens to the theory, you'll get the main point and have a good blueprint of how it is supported so that you can go back efficiently to any important details.

LESSON

HOMEWORK

Passage 5

It is hard to find a politician who doesn't have some sort of plan for energy independence, but we will never see true independence from foreign sources of energy without making the kind of sacrifices that elected officials are loath to mention. For example, virtually every politician campaigning for national office touts biofuels, especially ethanol, as a solution to our nation's energy dependence. However, the actual energy that can be harvested from these sources is miniscule compared to our current level of consumption—about 20 million barrels of oil and gasoline per day.

We need to take serious, even drastic, steps now. Nuclear fuel, despite all its promise, is understandably controversial, and the problem of dealing with radioactive waste will not go away anytime soon. We might find an acceptable method of drilling for oil in environmentally sensitive areas such as the Alaskan wilderness, but this too will take some time, and will only take us so far down the road to energy independence.

Thus, it is the level of consumption, rather than our sources of energy, that needs to change; putting our resources into developing alternative energy sources will only obscure this unavoidable fact. One way policymakers might affect the level of energy consumption is by increasing taxes on gasoline. In accordance with the principles of a free-market economy, such as that of our own nation, if the price of gasoline were to double due to the addition of such taxes, oil consumption would drop by 3 to 5 million barrels per day.

We also need to overhaul the way in which we move goods around the country. Using gas-guzzling trucks for cross-country trips is extremely inefficient. Moving away from the use of trucks for long-haul trips will require significant governmental and private investment in new water transport and electric railway infrastructure. Once this infrastructure is in place, however, these methods of shipping will be much more energy efficient for all but local transportation of goods.

These and other real solutions to our energy dependence issues will be unpopular in many quarters. Car and truck manufacturers will use their considerable political muscle to fight not only significant gas tax hikes, but also stringent fuel efficiency requirements on vehicles. The move away from trucking will be resisted by both the "big-box" retail outlets, which depend on trucks for the delivery of goods, and by the trucking industry itself. The farming industry will do everything it can to push for the widespread use of ethanol and other plant-based fuels. But it is consumer resistance that most needs to be overcome. Too many of us believe that the guarantee of cheap fuel is an inalienable right, and balk at funding public transportation.

Recently, there has been a gradual change in attitude as people start to connect their daily habits with larger environmental concerns. Until enough of us make that connection and are willing to make a few lifestyle changes accordingly, we have no business complaining about our energy dependence on other countries.

18. What does the author of the passage believe is most important for lessening our need for foreign sources of energy?

   (A) The political courage of elected officials to make tough decisions

   (B) Civic responsibility on the part of the automotive industry

   (C) The willingness of consumers to change their habits

   (D) A restructuring of the farming and trucking industries

   (E) The development of safe alternatives to oil

Passage 5

It is hard to find a politician who doesn't have some sort of plan for energy independence, but we will never see true independence from foreign sources of energy without making the kind of sacrifices that elected officials are loath to mention. For example, virtually every politician campaigning for national office touts biofuels, especially ethanol, as a solution to our nation's energy dependence. However, the actual energy that can be harvested from these sources is miniscule compared to our current level of consumption—about 20 million barrels of oil and gasoline per day.

We need to take serious, even drastic, steps now. Nuclear fuel, despite all its promise, is understandably controversial, and the problem of dealing with radioactive waste will not go away anytime soon. We might find an acceptable method of drilling for oil in environmentally sensitive areas such as the Alaskan wilderness, but this too will take some time, and will only take us so far down the road to energy independence.

Thus, it is the level of consumption, rather than our sources of energy, that needs to change; putting our resources into developing alternative energy sources will only obscure this unavoidable fact. One way policymakers might affect the level of energy consumption is by increasing taxes on gasoline. In accordance with the principles of a free-market economy, such as that of our own nation, if the price of gasoline were to double due to the addition of such taxes, oil consumption would drop by 3 to 5 million barrels per day.

We also need to overhaul the way in which we move goods around the country. Using gas-guzzling trucks for cross-country trips is extremely inefficient. Moving away from the use of trucks for long-haul trips will require significant governmental and private investment in new water transport and electric railway infrastructure. Once this infrastructure is in place, however, these methods of shipping will be much more energy efficient for all but local transportation of goods.

These and other real solutions to our energy dependence issues will be unpopular in many quarters. Car and truck manufacturers will use their considerable political muscle to fight not only significant gas tax hikes, but also stringent fuel efficiency requirements on vehicles. The move away from trucking will be resisted by both the "big-box" retail outlets, which depend on trucks for the delivery of goods, and by the trucking industry itself. The farming industry will do everything it can to push for the widespread use of ethanol and other plant-based fuels. But it is consumer resistance that most needs to be overcome. Too many of us believe that the guarantee of cheap fuel is an inalienable right, and balk at funding public transportation.

Recently, there has been a gradual change in attitude as people start to connect their daily habits with larger environmental concerns. Until enough of us make that connection and are willing to make a few lifestyle changes accordingly, we have no business complaining about our energy dependence on other countries.

19. Which of the following best characterizes the author's opinion of ethanol?

(A) Despite its popularity with politicians, it will not have enough impact to substantially lessen our dependence on foreign sources of energy.

(B) The influence of the farming industry will prevent it from becoming available to most consumers.

(C) It is the most practical of the various plant-based biofuels available.

(D) Its use will play a small part in reducing our energy needs.

(E) It is unlikely to be useful as a way of our gaining energy independence because of consumer resistance to its use.

Passage 5

It is hard to find a politician who doesn't have some sort of plan for energy independence, but we will never see true independence from foreign sources of energy without making the kind of sacrifices that elected officials are loath to mention. For example, virtually every politician campaigning for national office touts biofuels, especially ethanol, as a solution to our nation's energy dependence. However, the actual energy that can be harvested from these sources is miniscule compared to our current level of consumption—about 20 million barrels of oil and gasoline per day.

We need to take serious, even drastic, steps now. Nuclear fuel, despite all its promise, is understandably controversial, and the problem of dealing with radioactive waste will not go away anytime soon. We might find an acceptable method of drilling for oil in environmentally sensitive areas such as the Alaskan wilderness, but this too will take some time, and will only take us so far down the road to energy independence.

Thus, it is the level of consumption, rather than our sources of energy, that needs to change; putting our resources into developing alternative energy sources will only obscure this unavoidable fact. One way policymakers might affect the level of energy consumption is by increasing taxes on gasoline. In accordance with the principles of a free-market economy, such as that of our own nation, if the price of gasoline were to double due to the addition of such taxes, oil consumption would drop by 3 to 5 million barrels per day.

We also need to overhaul the way in which we move goods around the country. Using gas-guzzling trucks for cross-country trips is extremely inefficient. Moving away from the use of trucks for long-haul trips will require significant governmental and private investment in new water transport and electric railway infrastructure. Once this infrastructure is in place, however, these methods of shipping will be much more energy efficient for all but local transportation of goods.

These and other real solutions to our energy dependence issues will be unpopular in many quarters. Car and truck manufacturers will use their considerable political muscle to fight not only significant gas tax hikes, but also stringent fuel efficiency requirements on vehicles. The move away from trucking will be resisted by both the "big-box" retail outlets, which depend on trucks for the delivery of goods, and by the trucking industry itself. The farming industry will do everything it can to push for the widespread use of ethanol and other plant-based fuels. But it is consumer resistance that most needs to be overcome. Too many of us believe that the guarantee of cheap fuel is an inalienable right, and balk at funding public transportation.

Recently, there has been a gradual change in attitude as people start to connect their daily habits with larger environmental concerns. Until enough of us make that connection and are willing to make a few lifestyle changes accordingly, we have no business complaining about our energy dependence on other countries.

20. It can be inferred that the author believes that a tax increase on gasoline _____.

    (A) is not feasible because politicians do not understand the issue enough to call for such a raise

    (B) will limit the transporting of goods by "big-box" retail outlets

    (C) will reduce our annual consumption by approximately 4 million gallons

    (D) will only be possible after improvements have been made in automobile fuel efficiency

    (E) will use the fundamentals of free-market economics to address the problem of energy dependence

Passage 5

It is hard to find a politician who doesn't have some sort of plan for energy independence, but we will never see true independence from foreign sources of energy without making the kind of sacrifices that elected officials are loath to mention. For example, virtually every politician campaigning for national office touts biofuels, especially ethanol, as a solution to our nation's energy dependence. However, the actual energy that can be harvested from these sources is miniscule compared to our current level of consumption—about 20 million barrels of oil and gasoline per day.

We need to take serious, even drastic, steps now. Nuclear fuel, despite all its promise, is understandably controversial, and the problem of dealing with radioactive waste will not go away anytime soon. We might find an acceptable method of drilling for oil in environmentally sensitive areas such as the Alaskan wilderness, but this too will take some time, and will only take us so far down the road to energy independence.

Thus, it is the level of consumption, rather than our sources of energy, that needs to change; putting our resources into developing alternative energy sources will only obscure this unavoidable fact. One way policymakers might affect the level of energy consumption is by increasing taxes on gasoline. In accordance with the principles of a free-market economy, such as that of our own nation, if the price of gasoline were to double due to the addition of such taxes, oil consumption would drop by 3 to 5 million barrels per day.

We also need to overhaul the way in which we move goods around the country. Using gas-guzzling trucks for cross-country trips is extremely inefficient. Moving away from the use of trucks for long-haul trips will require significant governmental and private investment in new water transport and electric railway infrastructure. Once this infrastructure is in place, however, these methods of shipping will be much more energy efficient for all but local transportation of goods.

These and other real solutions to our energy dependence issues will be unpopular in many quarters. Car and truck manufacturers will use their considerable political muscle to fight not only significant gas tax hikes, but also stringent fuel efficiency requirements on vehicles. The move away from trucking will be resisted by both the "big-box" retail outlets, which depend on trucks for the delivery of goods, and by the trucking industry itself. The farming industry will do everything it can to push for the widespread use of ethanol and other plant-based fuels. But it is consumer resistance that most needs to be overcome. Too many of us believe that the guarantee of cheap fuel is an inalienable right, and balk at funding public transportation.

Recently, there has been a gradual change in attitude as people start to connect their daily habits with larger environmental concerns. Until enough of us make that connection and are willing to make a few lifestyle changes accordingly, we have no business complaining about our energy dependence on other countries.

21. The primary purpose of the second paragraph of the passage is to _____.

   (A) dismiss some alternative forms of energy that are unpopular with big business

   (B) show that there are not enough new alternatives for becoming less dependent on foreign sources of energy

   (C) provide historical background for the problem of energy-dependence

   (D) show the problems inherent in two sources of energy that could help us be come more energy-independent

   (E) ridicule any attempt to solve the problem of energy-dependence that does not take into account consumption levels

Passage 6

Given the increasing popularity of online brokerage firms, the fact that these firms have started to offer their clients other financial services is hardly surprising. In some cases, customers can simply link their online stock portfolios with traditional accounts held by other financial institutions. More and more online brokers, however, offer their own interest-bearing checking accounts, money market accounts, and retirement accounts, and even provide mortgages and home equity loans.

Some investors are understandably attracted to the idea of a one-stop shop for all their financial needs, and indeed there are conveniences to having one's various asset accounts linked together. But consumer advocates point out that this convenience extends to criminals intent on gaining access to funds and financial data. As Francis Golsen of the Investor Protection Bureau points out, "Combining your assets at one financial institution is a bit like using your parked car to store your jewelry. If you become a victim of theft, there's that much more to thieve."

Another danger is that investors may be less selective when deciding which financial institution to use for various services, given that the easiest choice is to use one company for every service. The temptation not to shop around may lead to a hasty decision. This fact is not lost on brokerage firms, whose marketing departments are quick to take advantage of the cross-selling potential inherent in offering so many products. As a result, those who use one-stop banking should expect an increase in promotional material clogging their email inboxes.

To be fair, we are now seeing some very attractive products as more brokers get into the act of providing additional services. Some firms are offering checking accounts with interest rates so high that these accounts are most likely "loss leaders" designed to get investors interested in other financial products offered by the firm. But this can only last so long. No investor should assume that their beloved brokerage house, which now advertises free trading and checking accounts with interest rates of 3.9% (and no minimum balance required!) will continue to provide these offers a month after they were first made.

22. Which of the following is NOT mentioned in the passage as a possible negative result of "one-stop" banking?

    (A) The potential for criminal wrongdoing is heightened.

    (B) Investors may not sufficiently explore their options.

    (C) Investors may receive unwanted marketing offers.

    (D) Brokerage firms may lack sufficient expertise in managing other financial services such as mortgages and home equity loans.

    (E) Investors may wrongly assume that certain introductory offers are still in place.

Passage 6

Given the increasing popularity of online brokerage firms, the fact that these firms have started to offer their clients other financial services is hardly surprising. In some cases, customers can simply link their online stock portfolios with traditional accounts held by other financial institutions. More and more online brokers, however, offer their own interest-bearing checking accounts, money market accounts, and retirement accounts, and even provide mortgages and home equity loans.

Some investors are understandably attracted to the idea of a one-stop shop for all their financial needs, and indeed there are conveniences to having one's various asset accounts linked together. But consumer advocates point out that this convenience extends to criminals intent on gaining access to funds and financial data. As Francis Golsen of the Investor Protection Bureau points out, "Combining your assets at one financial institution is a bit like using your parked car to store your jewelry. If you become a victim of theft, there's that much more to thieve."

Another danger is that investors may be less selective when deciding which financial institution to use for various services, given that the easiest choice is to use one company for every service. The temptation not to shop around may lead to a hasty decision. This fact is not lost on brokerage firms, whose marketing departments are quick to take advantage of the cross-selling potential inherent in offering so many products. As a result, those who use one-stop banking should expect an increase in promotional material clogging their email inboxes.

To be fair, we are now seeing some very attractive products as more brokers get into the act of providing additional services. Some firms are offering checking accounts with interest rates so high that these accounts are most likely "loss leaders" designed to get investors interested in other financial products offered by the firm. But this can only last so long. No investor should assume that their beloved brokerage house, which now advertises free trading and checking accounts with interest rates of 3.9% (and no minimum balance required!) will continue to provide these offers a month after they were first made.

23. The primary purpose of the passage is to _____.

    (A) alert readers to certain risks associated with using "one-stop" shopping for financial needs

    (B) give examples of the ways in which online brokers have diversified their services

    (C) raise questions about the legitimacy of cross-selling financial services

    (D) advise investors not to link traditional bank accounts with online accounts

    (E) provide an overview of recent changes in online brokering

Passage 6

Given the increasing popularity of online brokerage firms, the fact that these firms have started to offer their clients other financial services is hardly surprising. In some cases, customers can simply link their online stock portfolios with traditional accounts held by other financial institutions. More and more online brokers, however, offer their own interest-bearing checking accounts, money market accounts, and retirement accounts, and even provide mortgages and home equity loans.

Some investors are understandably attracted to the idea of a one-stop shop for all their financial needs, and indeed there are conveniences to having one's various asset accounts linked together. But consumer advocates point out that this convenience extends to criminals intent on gaining access to funds and financial data. As Francis Golsen of the Investor Protection Bureau points out, "Combining your assets at one financial institution is a bit like using your parked car to store your jewelry. If you become a victim of theft, there's that much more to thieve."

Another danger is that investors may be less selective when deciding which financial institution to use for various services, given that the easiest choice is to use one company for every service. The temptation not to shop around may lead to a hasty decision. This fact is not lost on brokerage firms, whose marketing departments are quick to take advantage of the cross-selling potential inherent in offering so many products. As a result, those who use one-stop banking should expect an increase in promotional material clogging their email inboxes.

To be fair, we are now seeing some very attractive products as more brokers get into the act of providing additional services. Some firms are offering checking accounts with interest rates so high that these accounts are most likely "loss leaders" designed to get investors interested in other financial products offered by the firm. But this can only last so long. No investor should assume that their beloved brokerage house, which now advertises free trading and checking accounts with interest rates of 3.9% (and no minimum balance required!) will continue to provide these offers a month after they were first made.

24. It can be inferred from the passage that the increase in the number of online brokers who offer banking services _____.

(A) was a result of consumer dissatisfaction with the level of service offered by traditional banks

(B) could come to an abrupt end without much warning

(C) has led to some financial products that appear to be very desirable to investors

(D) has contributed to an increase in the number of crimes involving the theft of financial data

(E) is, despite some risks, generally beneficial to investors who want to diversify their stock portfolios

Passage 6

Given the increasing popularity of online brokerage firms, the fact that these firms have started to offer their clients other financial services is hardly surprising. In some cases, customers can simply link their online stock portfolios with traditional accounts held by other financial institutions. More and more online brokers, however, offer their own interest-bearing checking accounts, money market accounts, and retirement accounts, and even provide mortgages and home equity loans.

Some investors are understandably attracted to the idea of a one-stop shop for all their financial needs, and indeed there are conveniences to having one's various asset accounts linked together. But consumer advocates point out that this convenience extends to criminals intent on gaining access to funds and financial data. As Francis Golsen of the Investor Protection Bureau points out, "Combining your assets at one financial institution is a bit like using your parked car to store your jewelry. If you become a victim of theft, there's that much more to thieve."

Another danger is that investors may be less selective when deciding which financial institution to use for various services, given that the easiest choice is to use one company for every service. The temptation not to shop around may lead to a hasty decision. This fact is not lost on brokerage firms, whose marketing departments are quick to take advantage of the cross-selling potential inherent in offering so many products. As a result, those who use one-stop banking should expect an increase in promotional material clogging their email inboxes.

To be fair, we are now seeing some very attractive products as more brokers get into the act of providing additional services. Some firms are offering checking accounts with interest rates so high that these accounts are most likely "loss leaders" designed to get investors interested in other financial products offered by the firm. But this can only last so long. No investor should assume that their beloved brokerage house, which now advertises free trading and checking accounts with interest rates of 3.9% (and no minimum balance required!) will continue to provide these offers a month after they were first made.

25. The purpose of the second paragraph is to make which of the following points?

    (A) Linking many of one's financial assets is risky and no more convenient than keeping one's banking and online portfolios separate.

    (B) One-stop banking puts investors at risk for more than just theft of assets and   financial data.

    (C) Using one firm for many financial services puts one at a greater risk of theft than using several institutions does.

    (D) Investors who use their online broker for diverse banking services risk making hasty financial decisions.

    (E) Traditional banking services such as mortgages are best provided by traditional banks.

Passage 7

Archaeologists working in two recently discovered limestone caves in Sarawak, Malaysia have found a surprising collection of 51 paintings estimated to be 6,000 to 12,000 years old. The paintings are unusual in their medium, manner of display, and subject matter. These are not simply wall or ceiling paintings. Stones—some as small as notebooks, some as large as doors—have been chipped and otherwise shaped to form rough canvases on which are painted individual works. Some of the pieces are stacked, while others are arranged upright in an overlapping pattern so that one can "flip through" the smaller pieces in the collection with relative ease. Hunters, warriors, and hunted animals, the typical subjects of cave art, are largely absent from these works. Instead, domestic scenes are represented, including food preparations, family meals, and recreational activities.

Though no tools have been found in the area, the fineness of the lines suggests the use of sophisticated animal-hair brushes. Gypsum, manganese, malachite, and other minerals were painstakingly ground and mixed with binding materials such as vegetable and animal oils to form the paints. In some cases, the artist or artists (Dr. Linus Mendoza of the International Speleologist Association has studied the paintings and believes that stylistic similarities and differences point to the work of three artists) have removed the patina surrounding the intended figures, producing a negative image. One probable reason for the high level of artistry is that the paintings may have been produced in the open air, where the light was good, and then brought into the cave.

However, it is the purpose of the paintings that is the most curious. Conventional wisdom holds that the hunting scenes found in cave art were meant to provide super-natural aid during actual hunts, or that figures and designs were painted by prehistoric shamans as a way of drawing power from the cave itself. It may also be that the scenes of domestic life are, like representations of hunting, meant to ensure good luck. Though facial features are rarely distinct, the paintings do suggest contentedness, or at least an absence of conflict. Most tantalizingly, it may be that the collection represents a sort of family tree. A number of the paintings appear to feature some of the same people, and it is tempting to think of these works as family portraits. Indeed, one figure, seen as a child with a mark on its forehead—the stone has actually been chipped away to represent the mark—is shown in other paintings as a young person and as an adult with the same mark.

26. Which of the following is mentioned in the passage as an unusual feature of the stone paintings?

    (A) The high level of artistry

    (B) The age of the paintings

    (C) The range in the size of the figures in the painting

    (D) The lack of distinct facial features

    (E) The overlapping presentation of the pieces

Passage 7

Archaeologists working in two recently discovered limestone caves in Sarawak, Malaysia have found a surprising collection of 51 paintings estimated to be 6,000 to 12,000 years old. The paintings are unusual in their medium, manner of display, and subject matter. These are not simply wall or ceiling paintings. Stones—some as small as notebooks, some as large as doors—have been chipped and otherwise shaped to form rough canvases on which are painted individual works. Some of the pieces are stacked, while others are arranged upright in an overlapping pattern so that one can "flip through" the smaller pieces in the collection with relative ease. Hunters, warriors, and hunted animals, the typical subjects of cave art, are largely absent from these works. Instead, domestic scenes are represented, including food preparations, family meals, and recreational activities.

Though no tools have been found in the area, the fineness of the lines suggests the use of sophisticated animal-hair brushes. Gypsum, manganese, malachite, and other minerals were painstakingly ground and mixed with binding materials such as vegetable and animal oils to form the paints. In some cases, the artist or artists (Dr. Linus Mendoza of the International Speleologist Association has studied the paintings and believes that stylistic similarities and differences point to the work of three artists) have removed the patina surrounding the intended figures, producing a negative image. One probable reason for the high level of artistry is that the paintings may have been produced in the open air, where the light was good, and then brought into the cave.

However, it is the purpose of the paintings that is the most curious. Conventional wisdom holds that the hunting scenes found in cave art were meant to provide super-natural aid during actual hunts, or that figures and designs were painted by prehistoric shamans as a way of drawing power from the cave itself. It may also be that the scenes of domestic life are, like representations of hunting, meant to ensure good luck. Though facial features are rarely distinct, the paintings do suggest contentedness, or at least an absence of conflict. Most tantalizingly, it may be that the collection represents a sort of family tree. A number of the paintings appear to feature some of the same people, and it is tempting to think of these works as family portraits. Indeed, one figure, seen as a child with a mark on its forehead—the stone has actually been chipped away to represent the mark—is shown in other paintings as a young person and as an adult with the same mark.

27. The author of the passage is especially interested in _____.

    (A) the possibility that the paintings trace the lineage of a family

    (B) the manner in which the paints were made

    (C) the stylistic differences exhibited in the paintings

    (D) the location of the caves in which the stone paintings were discovered

    (E) the method by which negative images were created

Passage 7

Archaeologists working in two recently discovered limestone caves in Sarawak, Malaysia have found a surprising collection of 51 paintings estimated to be 6,000 to 12,000 years old. The paintings are unusual in their medium, manner of display, and subject matter. These are not simply wall or ceiling paintings. Stones—some as small as notebooks, some as large as doors—have been chipped and otherwise shaped to form rough canvases on which are painted individual works. Some of the pieces are stacked, while others are arranged upright in an overlapping pattern so that one can "flip through" the smaller pieces in the collection with relative ease. Hunters, warriors, and hunted animals, the typical subjects of cave art, are largely absent from these works. Instead, domestic scenes are represented, including food preparations, family meals, and recreational activities.

Though no tools have been found in the area, the fineness of the lines suggests the use of sophisticated animal-hair brushes. Gypsum, manganese, malachite, and other minerals were painstakingly ground and mixed with binding materials such as vegetable and animal oils to form the paints. In some cases, the artist or artists (Dr. Linus Mendoza of the International Speleologist Association has studied the paintings and believes that stylistic similarities and differences point to the work of three artists) have removed the patina surrounding the intended figures, producing a negative image. One probable reason for the high level of artistry is that the paintings may have been produced in the open air, where the light was good, and then brought into the cave.

However, it is the purpose of the paintings that is the most curious. Conventional wisdom holds that the hunting scenes found in cave art were meant to provide super-natural aid during actual hunts, or that figures and designs were painted by prehistoric shamans as a way of drawing power from the cave itself. It may also be that the scenes of domestic life are, like representations of hunting, meant to ensure good luck. Though facial features are rarely distinct, the paintings do suggest contentedness, or at least an absence of conflict. Most tantalizingly, it may be that the collection represents a sort of family tree. A number of the paintings appear to feature some of the same people, and it is tempting to think of these works as family portraits. Indeed, one figure, seen as a child with a mark on its forehead—the stone has actually been chipped away to represent the mark—is shown in other paintings as a young person and as an adult with the same mark.

28. The primary purpose of the passage is to _____.

   (A) present an overview of stone paintings and show how they differ from most cave paintings

   (B) offer evidence that the stone paintings found in Sarawak most likely represent a family tree

   (C) detail some of the reasons that the discovery of the stone paintings is of considerable interest

   (D) persuade the reader of the great skill that went into the creation of the stone paintings

   (E) discuss the reasons that prehistoric people created cave art and stone art

Passage 7

Archaeologists working in two recently discovered limestone caves in Sarawak, Malaysia have found a surprising collection of 51 paintings estimated to be 6,000 to 12,000 years old. The paintings are unusual in their medium, manner of display, and subject matter. These are not simply wall or ceiling paintings. Stones—some as small as notebooks, some as large as doors—have been chipped and otherwise shaped to form rough canvases on which are painted individual works. Some of the pieces are stacked, while others are arranged upright in an overlapping pattern so that one can "flip through" the smaller pieces in the collection with relative ease. Hunters, warriors, and hunted animals, the typical subjects of cave art, are largely absent from these works. Instead, domestic scenes are represented, including food preparations, family meals, and recreational activities.

Though no tools have been found in the area, the fineness of the lines suggests the use of sophisticated animal-hair brushes. Gypsum, manganese, malachite, and other minerals were painstakingly ground and mixed with binding materials such as vegetable and animal oils to form the paints. In some cases, the artist or artists (Dr. Linus Mendoza of the International Speleologist Association has studied the paintings and believes that stylistic similarities and differences point to the work of three artists) have removed the patina surrounding the intended figures, producing a negative image. One probable reason for the high level of artistry is that the paintings may have been produced in the open air, where the light was good, and then brought into the cave.

However, it is the purpose of the paintings that is the most curious. Conventional wisdom holds that the hunting scenes found in cave art were meant to provide super-natural aid during actual hunts, or that figures and designs were painted by prehistoric shamans as a way of drawing power from the cave itself. It may also be that the scenes of domestic life are, like representations of hunting, meant to ensure good luck. Though facial features are rarely distinct, the paintings do suggest contentedness, or at least an absence of conflict. Most tantalizingly, it may be that the collection represents a sort of family tree. A number of the paintings appear to feature some of the same people, and it is tempting to think of these works as family portraits. Indeed, one figure, seen as a child with a mark on its forehead—the stone has actually been chipped away to represent the mark—is shown in other paintings as a young person and as an adult with the same mark.

29. Which of the following, if true, would most undermine a possibility mentioned by the author of the passage?

   (A) The use of brushes made from animal hair did not become a common practice until about 6,000 years ago.

   (B) Stones found in a nearby cave have been painted exclusively with animal figures.

   (C) A chemical analysis shows that some of the paintings contain no gypsum, manganese, or malachite.

   (D) To show that someone had died at the approximate age shown in a painting, the artists who created the stone paintings made a mark on the head of the figure by chipping the stone.

   (E) Carbon-dating reveals that the stone paintings were created over a period of 200 years.

Passage 8

A new study by the American Seller Institute (ASI) has tried to pin down, with scientific precision, the personal qualities that contribute to superior selling. Over a period of three years, the financial ups and downs of twelve sales teams in ten different fields were carefully tracked. The 75 salespeople involved were analyzed and tested for various personal and even physical characteristics. Interviews were conducted with family members and with people who bought (or did not buy) the salespeople's products. The results have been published by ASI in *The Selling Quality*, a 620-page work filled with as many bar graphs as anecdotes from the road.

Three personality types emerge as characteristic of the most successful sellers. The Chameleon, as the name implies, is adept at quickly understanding how clients see themselves (or would like to see themselves), and then mirroring that image. A good Chameleon is highly attentive, shrewd, and often unaware of what he or she is doing. This personality is formed early in life, and its attributes are hard to acquire. The Chameleon, perhaps because of strong mediating skills, often has a happy domestic life.

The Charismatic, in contrast, relies on a strong, even intimidating physical presence, as an essential tool to close a sale. Charismatics reverse the typical dynamic between seller and buyer, convincing clients that they should please the seller, and that the seller has something of great worth that the client needs to ask for. These people have, as *The Selling Quality* puts it, a "productive self-centeredness" that often leads to management positions, but also to less stability at home. Like the Chameleon, the Charismatic has traits that are seen early in life and that are difficult to cultivate in adulthood.

The Student—the third successful sales personality type—literally does his or her homework. An ability to provide useful data at a moment's notice and a relatively mild persona make the Student a highly effective collaborator with a Charismatic. Students have risen to management positions through persistence and an ability to see where an industry is headed, but a lack of leadership skills often keeps them out of top positions. While the skills of a top-notch Student seller are based less on intuition than are those of the other selling types, studying trade publications and mapping out a would-be client company's hierarchy are not enough to make a Student a superior salesperson. An ability to communicate a genuine (or seemingly genuine) enthusiasm for the product is crucial to a Student's success, as it is for all successful sellers.

30. The primary purpose of this passage is to _____.

    (A) provide the reader with a recommendation

    (B) summarize and critique the contents of a book of non-fiction

    (C) give an overview of some of the findings of a new study

    (D) propose a system for categorizing the workers in a given field

    (E) report on a ranking of three personality types

Passage 8

A new study by the American Seller Institute (ASI) has tried to pin down, with scientific precision, the personal qualities that contribute to superior selling. Over a period of three years, the financial ups and downs of twelve sales teams in ten different fields were carefully tracked. The 75 salespeople involved were analyzed and tested for various personal and even physical characteristics. Interviews were conducted with family members and with people who bought (or did not buy) the salespeople's products. The results have been published by ASI in *The Selling Quality*, a 620-page work filled with as many bar graphs as anecdotes from the road.

Three personality types emerge as characteristic of the most successful sellers. The Chameleon, as the name implies, is adept at quickly understanding how clients see themselves (or would like to see themselves), and then mirroring that image. A good Chameleon is highly attentive, shrewd, and often unaware of what he or she is doing. This personality is formed early in life, and its attributes are hard to acquire. The Chameleon, perhaps because of strong mediating skills, often has a happy domestic life.

The Charismatic, in contrast, relies on a strong, even intimidating physical presence, as an essential tool to close a sale. Charismatics reverse the typical dynamic between seller and buyer, convincing clients that they should please the seller, and that the seller has something of great worth that the client needs to ask for. These people have, as *The Selling Quality* puts it, a "productive self-centeredness" that often leads to management positions, but also to less stability at home. Like the Chameleon, the Charismatic has traits that are seen early in life and that are difficult to cultivate in adulthood.

The Student—the third successful sales personality type—literally does his or her homework. An ability to provide useful data at a moment's notice and a relatively mild persona make the Student a highly effective collaborator with a Charismatic. Students have risen to management positions through persistence and an ability to see where an industry is headed, but a lack of leadership skills often keeps them out of top positions. While the skills of a top-notch Student seller are based less on intuition than are those of the other selling types, studying trade publications and mapping out a would-be client company's hierarchy are not enough to make a Student a superior salesperson. An ability to communicate a genuine (or seemingly genuine) enthusiasm for the product is crucial to a Student's success, as it is for all successful sellers.

31. According to the passage, *The Selling Quality* implies that Students, in comparison with Chameleons and Charismatics, _____.

    (A) are generally not as successful

    (B) tend to have stable domestic lives

    (C) rely exclusively on their ability to research their fields

    (D) have skills that are more easily acquired

    (E) rise to management positions for which they are not well suited

Passage 8

A new study by the American Seller Institute (ASI) has tried to pin down, with scientific precision, the personal qualities that contribute to superior selling. Over a period of three years, the financial ups and downs of twelve sales teams in ten different fields were carefully tracked. The 75 salespeople involved were analyzed and tested for various personal and even physical characteristics. Interviews were conducted with family members and with people who bought (or did not buy) the salespeople's products. The results have been published by ASI in *The Selling Quality*, a 620-page work filled with as many bar graphs as anecdotes from the road.

Three personality types emerge as characteristic of the most successful sellers. The Chameleon, as the name implies, is adept at quickly understanding how clients see themselves (or would like to see themselves), and then mirroring that image. A good Chameleon is highly attentive, shrewd, and often unaware of what he or she is doing. This personality is formed early in life, and its attributes are hard to acquire. The Chameleon, perhaps because of strong mediating skills, often has a happy domestic life.

The Charismatic, in contrast, relies on a strong, even intimidating physical presence, as an essential tool to close a sale. Charismatics reverse the typical dynamic between seller and buyer, convincing clients that they should please the seller, and that the seller has something of great worth that the client needs to ask for. These people have, as *The Selling Quality* puts it, a "productive self-centeredness" that often leads to management positions, but also to less stability at home. Like the Chameleon, the Charismatic has traits that are seen early in life and that are difficult to cultivate in adulthood.

The Student—the third successful sales personality type—literally does his or her homework. An ability to provide useful data at a moment's notice and a relatively mild persona make the Student a highly effective collaborator with a Charismatic. Students have risen to management positions through persistence and an ability to see where an industry is headed, but a lack of leadership skills often keeps them out of top positions. While the skills of a top-notch Student seller are based less on intuition than are those of the other selling types, studying trade publications and mapping out a would-be client company's hierarchy are not enough to make a Student a superior salesperson. An ability to communicate a genuine (or seemingly genuine) enthusiasm for the product is crucial to a Student's success, as it is for all successful sellers.

32. What does the author assume about the usual relationship between buyer and seller?

   (A) The buyer is generally unaware of the methods of a successful seller.

   (B) The seller is in a position of less control.

   (C) The successful seller knows more about the product than does the buyer.

   (D) A high degree of trust between both parties is crucial for the formation of a successful relationship.

   (E) The seller is less convinced of the worth of the product than is the buyer.

Passage 8

A new study by the American Seller Institute (ASI) has tried to pin down, with scientific precision, the personal qualities that contribute to superior selling. Over a period of three years, the financial ups and downs of twelve sales teams in ten different fields were carefully tracked. The 75 salespeople involved were analyzed and tested for various personal and even physical characteristics. Interviews were conducted with family members and with people who bought (or did not buy) the salespeople's products. The results have been published by ASI in *The Selling Quality*, a 620-page work filled with as many bar graphs as anecdotes from the road.

Three personality types emerge as characteristic of the most successful sellers. The Chameleon, as the name implies, is adept at quickly understanding how clients see themselves (or would like to see themselves), and then mirroring that image. A good Chameleon is highly attentive, shrewd, and often unaware of what he or she is doing. This personality is formed early in life, and its attributes are hard to acquire. The Chameleon, perhaps because of strong mediating skills, often has a happy domestic life.

The Charismatic, in contrast, relies on a strong, even intimidating physical presence, as an essential tool to close a sale. Charismatics reverse the typical dynamic between seller and buyer, convincing clients that they should please the seller, and that the seller has something of great worth that the client needs to ask for. These people have, as *The Selling Quality* puts it, a "productive self-centeredness" that often leads to management positions, but also to less stability at home. Like the Chameleon, the Charismatic has traits that are seen early in life and that are difficult to cultivate in adulthood.

The Student—the third successful sales personality type—literally does his or her homework. An ability to provide useful data at a moment's notice and a relatively mild persona make the Student a highly effective collaborator with a Charismatic. Students have risen to management positions through persistence and an ability to see where an industry is headed, but a lack of leadership skills often keeps them out of top positions. While the skills of a top-notch Student seller are based less on intuition than are those of the other selling types, studying trade publications and mapping out a would-be client company's hierarchy are not enough to make a Student a superior salesperson. An ability to communicate a genuine (or seemingly genuine) enthusiasm for the product is crucial to a Student's success, as it is for all successful sellers.

33. Which of the following is implied about Chameleons?

    (A) They are highly organized.

    (B) They rarely rise to top management positions.

    (C) They are skilled at resolving disputes.

    (D) They tend to marry people similar to themselves.

    (E) They generally do more research on their client than do Charismatics.

Passage 8

A new study by the American Seller Institute (ASI) has tried to pin down, with scientific precision, the personal qualities that contribute to superior selling. Over a period of three years, the financial ups and downs of twelve sales teams in ten different fields were carefully tracked. The 75 salespeople involved were analyzed and tested for various personal and even physical characteristics. Interviews were conducted with family members and with people who bought (or did not buy) the salespeople's products. The results have been published by ASI in *The Selling Quality*, a 620-page work filled with as many bar graphs as anecdotes from the road.

Three personality types emerge as characteristic of the most successful sellers. The Chameleon, as the name implies, is adept at quickly understanding how clients see themselves (or would like to see themselves), and then mirroring that image. A good Chameleon is highly attentive, shrewd, and often unaware of what he or she is doing. This personality is formed early in life, and its attributes are hard to acquire. The Chameleon, perhaps because of strong mediating skills, often has a happy domestic life.

The Charismatic, in contrast, relies on a strong, even intimidating physical presence, as an essential tool to close a sale. Charismatics reverse the typical dynamic between seller and buyer, convincing clients that they should please the seller, and that the seller has something of great worth that the client needs to ask for. These people have, as *The Selling Quality* puts it, a "productive self-centeredness" that often leads to management positions, but also to less stability at home. Like the Chameleon, the Charismatic has traits that are seen early in life and that are difficult to cultivate in adulthood.

The Student—the third successful sales personality type—literally does his or her homework. An ability to provide useful data at a moment's notice and a relatively mild persona make the Student a highly effective collaborator with a Charismatic. Students have risen to management positions through persistence and an ability to see where an industry is headed, but a lack of leadership skills often keeps them out of top positions. While the skills of a top-notch Student seller are based less on intuition than are those of the other selling types, studying trade publications and mapping out a would-be client company's hierarchy are not enough to make a Student a superior salesperson. An ability to communicate a genuine (or seemingly genuine) enthusiasm for the product is crucial to a Student's success, as it is for all successful sellers.

34. The passage does NOT state which of the following about successful salespeople?

    (A) The most successful ones tend to fall into one of three categories.

    (B) Communication skills are important.

    (C) Some are capable of advancing their careers and entering management positions.

    (D) Their selling approach goes through dramatic changes throughout their careers.

    (E) They often use a selling style that is a reflection of a longstanding personality trait.

Passage 9

Over the last decade, a number of businesses have experimented with giving regional offices greater leeway in making decisions that traditionally had been handed down from headquarters. Local retailers have been given the latitude to devise regional branding that differs substantially from the company's national image. In the corporate world, two offices within the same firm in the same state might have differing hiring practices, hierarchical structures, and a different set of job benefits. One nationwide high-technology firm went so far as to give each of its regional offices a turn at doing business for three weeks in which all but the most urgent communications with the head office were discouraged.

One case study, involving a company that offers automobile, homeowner, and office insurance at a dozen locations in the Midwest and the South, provides a lesson in the pitfalls and advantages of "added autonomy," as this approach is sometimes called. At first, regional managers were wary of taking on too much self-governance, despite personal assurances from the company's president. This hesitancy initially led to less initiative, precisely the opposite of what was intended. Aggravating matters, many of the top people in the national office felt psychologically uneasy loosening the controls, especially when they realized that local offices were communicating more than ever with one another not under the watchful eyes of the head office. However, this region-to-region sharing of concerns and ideas proved to be genuinely beneficial. A discussion between managers at the firm's Atlanta and Oklahoma City offices led them both to abandon a new policy for drivers with substandard records, a decision that in retrospect saved the company millions of dollars.

Some regional offices went too far or moved too swiftly. When the firm's Topeka office decided to step up its marketing efforts to home business owners, a manager thought to save time by using promotional material that was based largely on the company's homeowner's insurance material. Eventually, the home office's legal department discovered that certain terms that applied to the homeowner's insurance should have been removed from the home business material. By the time this discovery was made, the firm was forced to honor the terms that had been offered.

Despite problems with the retention of personnel at both the regional and national levels, the company has decided to continue along with this program. In light of the company's slowed economic growth, the ability to find individuals who are comfortable with added autonomy may remain the biggest challenge to the program's proper implementation, for this or any other company that wishes to pursue an "added autonomy" initiative.

35. The passage is primarily concerned with which of the following?

    (A) Detailing the impact that a new business practice has had on several companies

    (B) Evaluating the unintended consequences of a shift in hiring and promoting practices at one representative business

    (C) Illustrating the importance of keeping lines of communication open between different offices within the same company

    (D) Providing a chronological outline of the impact of a new business model.

    (E) Reporting on a relatively recent phenomenon that has affected a variety of businesses

Passage 9

Over the last decade, a number of businesses have experimented with giving regional offices greater leeway in making decisions that traditionally had been handed down from headquarters. Local retailers have been given the latitude to devise regional branding that differs substantially from the company's national image. In the corporate world, two offices within the same firm in the same state might have differing hiring practices, hierarchical structures, and a different set of job benefits. One nationwide high-technology firm went so far as to give each of its regional offices a turn at doing business for three weeks in which all but the most urgent communications with the head office were discouraged.

One case study, involving a company that offers automobile, homeowner, and office insurance at a dozen locations in the Midwest and the South, provides a lesson in the pitfalls and advantages of "added autonomy," as this approach is sometimes called. At first, regional managers were wary of taking on too much self-governance, despite personal assurances from the company's president. This hesitancy initially led to less initiative, precisely the opposite of what was intended. Aggravating matters, many of the top people in the national office felt psychologically uneasy loosening the controls, especially when they realized that local offices were communicating more than ever with one another not under the watchful eyes of the head office. However, this region-to-region sharing of concerns and ideas proved to be genuinely beneficial. A discussion between managers at the firm's Atlanta and Oklahoma City offices led them both to abandon a new policy for drivers with substandard records, a decision that in retrospect saved the company millions of dollars.

Some regional offices went too far or moved too swiftly. When the firm's Topeka office decided to step up its marketing efforts to home business owners, a manager thought to save time by using promotional material that was based largely on the company's homeowner's insurance material. Eventually, the home office's legal department discovered that certain terms that applied to the homeowner's insurance should have been removed from the home business material. By the time this discovery was made, the firm was forced to honor the terms that had been offered.

Despite problems with the retention of personnel at both the regional and national levels, the company has decided to continue along with this program. In light of the company's slowed economic growth, the ability to find individuals who are comfortable with added autonomy may remain the biggest challenge to the program's proper implementation, for this or any other company that wishes to pursue an "added autonomy" initiative.

36. According to the passage, some regional managers of the insurance company who had been given added autonomy _____.

    (A) reported to the head office only when a crisis developed

    (B) were afraid to overstep the traditional limitations of their decision-making authority

    (C) only began to take initiative after receiving personal assurances from the company's president

    (D) depended on other regional managers for guidance and supervision

    (E) misinterpreted the intent of the new system.

Passage 9

Over the last decade, a number of businesses have experimented with giving regional offices greater leeway in making decisions that traditionally had been handed down from headquarters. Local retailers have been given the latitude to devise regional branding that differs substantially from the company's national image. In the corporate world, two offices within the same firm in the same state might have differing hiring practices, hierarchical structures, and a different set of job benefits. One nationwide high-technology firm went so far as to give each of its regional offices a turn at doing business for three weeks in which all but the most urgent communications with the head office were discouraged.

One case study, involving a company that offers automobile, homeowner, and office insurance at a dozen locations in the Midwest and the South, provides a lesson in the pitfalls and advantages of "added autonomy," as this approach is sometimes called. At first, regional managers were wary of taking on too much self-governance, despite personal assurances from the company's president. This hesitancy initially led to less initiative, precisely the opposite of what was intended. Aggravating matters, many of the top people in the national office felt psychologically uneasy loosening the controls, especially when they realized that local offices were communicating more than ever with one another not under the watchful eyes of the head office. However, this region-to-region sharing of concerns and ideas proved to be genuinely beneficial. A discussion between managers at the firm's Atlanta and Oklahoma City offices led them both to abandon a new policy for drivers with substandard records, a decision that in retrospect saved the company millions of dollars.

Some regional offices went too far or moved too swiftly. When the firm's Topeka office decided to step up its marketing efforts to home business owners, a manager thought to save time by using promotional material that was based largely on the company's homeowner's insurance material. Eventually, the home office's legal department discovered that certain terms that applied to the homeowner's insurance should have been removed from the home business material. By the time this discovery was made, the firm was forced to honor the terms that had been offered.

Despite problems with the retention of personnel at both the regional and national levels, the company has decided to continue along with this program. In light of the company's slowed economic growth, the ability to find individuals who are comfortable with added autonomy may remain the biggest challenge to the program's proper implementation, for this or any other company that wishes to pursue an "added autonomy" initiative.

37. Which of the following is most likely to be a result of a business implementing added autonomy?

   (A) The average age of a manager varies considerably among the various regional offices of a nationwide publishing firm.

   (B) A software manufacturer goes against the industry standard and intentionally doubles the time it takes to test new products before making them available to customers.

   (C) One branch of a clothing store distributes flyers that show a map of the store's location within the letters of the store's name, though no other branch displays the store's name this way.

   (D) A media company's president visits regional offices to meet with managers and offer face-to-face words of encouragement.

   (E) The success of a motorcycle manufacturer's sales team from one of its dealerships is published in the newsletter published by the company's head office.

Passage 9

Over the last decade, a number of businesses have experimented with giving regional offices greater leeway in making decisions that traditionally had been handed down from headquarters. Local retailers have been given the latitude to devise regional branding that differs substantially from the company's national image. In the corporate world, two offices within the same firm in the same state might have differing hiring practices, hierarchical structures, and a different set of job benefits. One nationwide high-technology firm went so far as to give each of its regional offices a turn at doing business for three weeks in which all but the most urgent communications with the head office were discouraged.

One case study, involving a company that offers automobile, homeowner, and office insurance at a dozen locations in the Midwest and the South, provides a lesson in the pitfalls and advantages of "added autonomy," as this approach is sometimes called. At first, regional managers were wary of taking on too much self-governance, despite personal assurances from the company's president. This hesitancy initially led to less initiative, precisely the opposite of what was intended. Aggravating matters, many of the top people in the national office felt psychologically uneasy loosening the controls, especially when they realized that local offices were communicating more than ever with one another not under the watchful eyes of the head office. However, this region-to-region sharing of concerns and ideas proved to be genuinely beneficial. A discussion between managers at the firm's Atlanta and Oklahoma City offices led them both to abandon a new policy for drivers with substandard records, a decision that in retrospect saved the company millions of dollars.

Some regional offices went too far or moved too swiftly. When the firm's Topeka office decided to step up its marketing efforts to home business owners, a manager thought to save time by using promotional material that was based largely on the company's homeowner's insurance material. Eventually, the home office's legal department discovered that certain terms that applied to the homeowner's insurance should have been removed from the home business material. By the time this discovery was made, the firm was forced to honor the terms that had been offered.

Despite problems with the retention of personnel at both the regional and national levels, the company has decided to continue along with this program. In light of the company's slowed economic growth, the ability to find individuals who are comfortable with added autonomy may remain the biggest challenge to the program's proper implementation, for this or any other company that wishes to pursue an "added autonomy" initiative.

38. Which of the following best describes the structure of the passage?

   (A) A problem is addressed, and then a solution is discussed through example and analysis.

   (B) A phenomenon is described, and then general examples are given, followed by a specific example that is discussed in some depth.

   (C) A business theory is outlined, and then several examples are given that show the inherent weakness of this theory.

   (D) A specific business model is analyzed, and the reasoning behind the model is gradually revealed.

   (E) The strengths of an idea are described and illustrated, followed by a description and illustration of the pitfalls of the idea.

Passage 10

After a slow start, Health Savings Accounts (HSAs)—tax-free savings accounts designed to help people save for their and their dependents' medical needs—have become increasingly popular with individuals who buy their own insurance, and with employers who provide it. The advantages of HSAs are fairly easy to understand: Funds placed into an HSA are sheltered from taxation, just as is the case with money put into Individual Retirement Accounts (IRAs). Unlike funds in IRAs, however, funds in HSAs (and earnings they have acquired through investments) are also exempt from taxation (and penalty) when they are taken out at any time, as long as the funds are used for medical purposes.

An HSA, however, must be combined with a high-deductible health plan. In addition, the amount that can be contributed annually to the account is restricted. Currently, an individual must have a deductible of at least $1,050 to participate, and can contribute as much as $2,700 per year. For families, the figures are higher. Because of the high deductible, out-of-pocket expenses can be substantial, though premiums are relatively low, making HSAs especially attractive to people who don't expect to need much medical care.

This last point is not lost on those who claim that low-income individuals with serious health issues are unlikely to derive any benefit from HSAs. If you don't make much, you will not be able to contribute much to the account. And because the deductible is so high, low earners will pay for a good deal of medical care before the deductible takes over. As a result, people who can't afford (in any sense) to gamble with their health may forego a trip to the doctor. Furthermore, since HSAs are increasingly perceived as attractive to relatively healthy and wealthy Americans, companies that provide traditional insurance may lose business and attempt to make up for this loss by raising their premiums or cutting benefits to low-income clients. Another argument against HSAs is the swelling effect that tax-free accounts will have on the national budget deficit.

No single initiative can solve this nation's health care problems. Many factors, including malpractice insurance, high-tech research costs, an aging population, and yes, old-fashioned greed, play a role in the rising cost of medical care. HSAs represent a move in the right direction, but they will almost certainly need to be adjusted and supplemented to make it easier for all individuals to get access to competent health care.

39. The passage is chiefly concerned with _____.

    (A) proving that HSAs are not yet sufficient to address the nation's health care problems

    (B) giving a balanced view of governmental approaches to making health care more affordable

    (C) making the point that HSAs, despite what critics have said, have become increasingly popular with individuals and employers

    (D) providing a basic understanding of HSAs, and presenting opinions on the subject, including those of the author

    (E) comparing HSAs to more traditional health insurance systems

Passage 10

After a slow start, Health Savings Accounts (HSAs)—tax-free savings accounts designed to help people save for their and their dependents' medical needs—have become increasingly popular with individuals who buy their own insurance, and with employers who provide it. The advantages of HSAs are fairly easy to understand: Funds placed into an HSA are sheltered from taxation, just as is the case with money put into Individual Retirement Accounts (IRAs). Unlike funds in IRAs, however, funds in HSAs (and earnings they have acquired through investments) are also exempt from taxation (and penalty) when they are taken out at any time, as long as the funds are used for medical purposes.

An HSA, however, must be combined with a high-deductible health plan. In addition, the amount that can be contributed annually to the account is restricted. Currently, an individual must have a deductible of at least $1,050 to participate, and can contribute as much as $2,700 per year. For families, the figures are higher. Because of the high deductible, out-of-pocket expenses can be substantial, though premiums are relatively low, making HSAs especially attractive to people who don't expect to need much medical care.

This last point is not lost on those who claim that low-income individuals with serious health issues are unlikely to derive any benefit from HSAs. If you don't make much, you will not be able to contribute much to the account. And because the deductible is so high, low earners will pay for a good deal of medical care before the deductible takes over. As a result, people who can't afford (in any sense) to gamble with their health may forego a trip to the doctor. Furthermore, since HSAs are increasingly perceived as attractive to relatively healthy and wealthy Americans, companies that provide traditional insurance may lose business and attempt to make up for this loss by raising their premiums or cutting benefits to low-income clients. Another argument against HSAs is the swelling effect that tax-free accounts will have on the national budget deficit.

No single initiative can solve this nation's health care problems. Many factors, including malpractice insurance, high-tech research costs, an aging population, and yes, old-fashioned greed, play a role in the rising cost of medical care. HSAs represent a move in the right direction, but they will almost certainly need to be adjusted and supplemented to make it easier for all individuals to get access to competent health care.

40. The last paragraph performs which of the following functions in the passage?

    (A) It presents a moderate view on the main topic and offers a generalized remedy for a relevant problem.

    (B) It summarizes the viewpoints expressed earlier in the passage.

    (C) It acknowledges that some problems are too complex to be completely solved.

    (D) It criticizes both of the main viewpoints that had been expressed earlier in the passage.

    (E) It offers statistical evidence to suggest that the problem discussed in the passage cannot be addressed through any one initiative.

Passage 10

After a slow start, Health Savings Accounts (HSAs)—tax-free savings accounts designed to help people save for their and their dependents' medical needs—have become increasingly popular with individuals who buy their own insurance, and with employers who provide it. The advantages of HSAs are fairly easy to understand: Funds placed into an HSA are sheltered from taxation, just as is the case with money put into Individual Retirement Accounts (IRAs). Unlike funds in IRAs, however, funds in HSAs (and earnings they have acquired through investments) are also exempt from taxation (and penalty) when they are taken out at any time, as long as the funds are used for medical purposes.

An HSA, however, must be combined with a high-deductible health plan. In addition, the amount that can be contributed annually to the account is restricted. Currently, an individual must have a deductible of at least $1,050 to participate, and can contribute as much as $2,700 per year. For families, the figures are higher. Because of the high deductible, out-of-pocket expenses can be substantial, though premiums are relatively low, making HSAs especially attractive to people who don't expect to need much medical care.

This last point is not lost on those who claim that low-income individuals with serious health issues are unlikely to derive any benefit from HSAs. If you don't make much, you will not be able to contribute much to the account. And because the deductible is so high, low earners will pay for a good deal of medical care before the deductible takes over. As a result, people who can't afford (in any sense) to gamble with their health may forego a trip to the doctor. Furthermore, since HSAs are increasingly perceived as attractive to relatively healthy and wealthy Americans, companies that provide traditional insurance may lose business and attempt to make up for this loss by raising their premiums or cutting benefits to low-income clients. Another argument against HSAs is the swelling effect that tax-free accounts will have on the national budget deficit.

No single initiative can solve this nation's health care problems. Many factors, including malpractice insurance, high-tech research costs, an aging population, and yes, old-fashioned greed, play a role in the rising cost of medical care. HSAs represent a move in the right direction, but they will almost certainly need to be adjusted and supplemented to make it easier for all individuals to get access to competent health care.

41. According to the passage, some critics of HSAs believe that _____.

   (A) those responsible for devising this type of account have not taken into consideration the effect it can have on the budget deficit

   (B) some people will not be able to put enough money into HSAs to make them worthwhile

   (C) only relatively healthy and wealthy individuals will sign up for one of these accounts

   (D) the relatively low premiums are still too high for many individuals

   (E) individuals who are interested in HSAs should not be forced to choose a high-deductible policy

Passage 10

After a slow start, Health Savings Accounts (HSAs)—tax-free savings accounts designed to help people save for their and their dependents' medical needs—have become increasingly popular with individuals who buy their own insurance, and with employers who provide it. The advantages of HSAs are fairly easy to understand: Funds placed into an HSA are sheltered from taxation, just as is the case with money put into Individual Retirement Accounts (IRAs). Unlike funds in IRAs, however, funds in HSAs (and earnings they have acquired through investments) are also exempt from taxation (and penalty) when they are taken out at any time, as long as the funds are used for medical purposes.

An HSA, however, must be combined with a high-deductible health plan. In addition, the amount that can be contributed annually to the account is restricted. Currently, an individual must have a deductible of at least $1,050 to participate, and can contribute as much as $2,700 per year. For families, the figures are higher. Because of the high deductible, out-of-pocket expenses can be substantial, though premiums are relatively low, making HSAs especially attractive to people who don't expect to need much medical care.

This last point is not lost on those who claim that low-income individuals with serious health issues are unlikely to derive any benefit from HSAs. If you don't make much, you will not be able to contribute much to the account. And because the deductible is so high, low earners will pay for a good deal of medical care before the deductible takes over. As a result, people who can't afford (in any sense) to gamble with their health may forego a trip to the doctor. Furthermore, since HSAs are increasingly perceived as attractive to relatively healthy and wealthy Americans, companies that provide traditional insurance may lose business and attempt to make up for this loss by raising their premiums or cutting benefits to low-income clients. Another argument against HSAs is the swelling effect that tax-free accounts will have on the national budget deficit.

No single initiative can solve this nation's health care problems. Many factors, including malpractice insurance, high-tech research costs, an aging population, and yes, old-fashioned greed, play a role in the rising cost of medical care. HSAs represent a move in the right direction, but they will almost certainly need to be adjusted and supplemented to make it easier for all individuals to get access to competent health care.

42. According to the passage, low-deductible policies _____.

   (A) offer several clear-cut advantages over HSAs

   (B) are limited by the quality of the health care they cover

   (C) have certain restrictions regarding how much they will cover in a given year

   (D) are offered by companies that are less motivated by greed than those that offer HSAs

   (E) may become increasingly expensive or less comprehensive

Passage 11

Relieving an impoverished country of its debt would seem to almost unavoidably help the citizens of that nation. Indeed, health care and education spending is now greater than debt service payments in many countries that have been granted partial debt relief by the Heavily Indebted Poor Countries (HIPC) Initiative launched by the International Monetary Fund and the World Bank, and complete debt relief by the supplementary Multilateral Debt Relief Initiative (MDRI). Several factors, however, have kept these programs from becoming truly transformational.

For a nation to qualify for the HIPC, it must have a level of debt that cannot be managed through traditional means. The removal of this enormous burden means that badly needed resources can go to programs that aid needy citizens, just as is intended. However, the HIPC has strict rules that sharply limit this spending. In some cases, teachers are not hired and HIV/AIDS tests are not administered because the sudden spending might lead to macroeconomic instability. This is a paradox that must be confronted: Poor nations need to spend money desperately but wisely.

A more daunting obstacle is the lack of a private sector in many of the countries that are served by the HIPC. Property rights may be virtually non-existent. Without individuals and businesses willing and able to invest resources in their own country, progress can be glacial. Outside investors are forced to deal not with business partners as such, but with governmental agencies ranging from the inept to the murderously corrupt. There is no guarantee that funds meant for a hospital or school will ever find their way to the intended destination, whether because of corruption or the sheer difficulty of moving goods around in a place that is, as is so often the case in truly poor countries, at war.

Debt relief remains an important tool in reducing the terrible suffering that affects so many people in the underdeveloped world. However, it is not enough to clean the slate and say, "start anew." Without the willingness on the part of the governing body to allow its citizens to take part in their own development, and without the right balance of emergency spending and careful investment, unmanageable debt will return, as evidenced by nations that have been borrowing money faster than their debt can be relieved.

43. Which of the following titles best summarizes the contents of the passage?

    (A) Debt Relief as a Tool for Increasing Private Investment in Impoverished Nations

    (B) The Difficulties of Implementing Debt Relief in Very Poor Countries

    (C) Obstacles to Channeling Aid to Needy Destinations in Very Poor Countries

    (D) The Inherent Flaws in Debt Relief Programs

    (E) HIPC: Well-Meaning, but Insufficient

Passage 11

Relieving an impoverished country of its debt would seem to almost unavoidably help the citizens of that nation. Indeed, health care and education spending is now greater than debt service payments in many countries that have been granted partial debt relief by the Heavily Indebted Poor Countries (HIPC) Initiative launched by the International Monetary Fund and the World Bank, and complete debt relief by the supplementary Multilateral Debt Relief Initiative (MDRI). Several factors, however, have kept these programs from becoming truly transformational.

For a nation to qualify for the HIPC, it must have a level of debt that cannot be managed through traditional means. The removal of this enormous burden means that badly needed resources can go to programs that aid needy citizens, just as is intended. However, the HIPC has strict rules that sharply limit this spending. In some cases, teachers are not hired and HIV/AIDS tests are not administered because the sudden spending might lead to macroeconomic instability. This is a paradox that must be confronted: Poor nations need to spend money desperately but wisely.

A more daunting obstacle is the lack of a private sector in many of the countries that are served by the HIPC. Property rights may be virtually non-existent. Without individuals and businesses willing and able to invest resources in their own country, progress can be glacial. Outside investors are forced to deal not with business partners as such, but with governmental agencies ranging from the inept to the murderously corrupt. There is no guarantee that funds meant for a hospital or school will ever find their way to the intended destination, whether because of corruption or the sheer difficulty of moving goods around in a place that is, as is so often the case in truly poor countries, at war.

Debt relief remains an important tool in reducing the terrible suffering that affects so many people in the underdeveloped world. However, it is not enough to clean the slate and say, "start anew." Without the willingness on the part of the governing body to allow its citizens to take part in their own development, and without the right balance of emergency spending and careful investment, unmanageable debt will return, as evidenced by nations that have been borrowing money faster than their debt can be relieved.

44. Which of the following was NOT mentioned as a difficulty associated with debt relief?

   (A) Long-term needs have to be addressed at the same time as more immediate one.

   (B) Nations that need debt relief are often in the midst of violent conflicts.

   (C) Debt relief can swiftly be replaced by new debt.

   (D) Private investors in very poor countries are often corrupt.

   (E) The pace of development in poor nations can be extremely slow.

Passage 11

Relieving an impoverished country of its debt would seem to almost unavoidably help the citizens of that nation. Indeed, health care and education spending is now greater than debt service payments in many countries that have been granted partial debt relief by the Heavily Indebted Poor Countries (HIPC) Initiative launched by the International Monetary Fund and the World Bank, and complete debt relief by the supplementary Multilateral Debt Relief Initiative (MDRI). Several factors, however, have kept these programs from becoming truly transformational.

For a nation to qualify for the HIPC, it must have a level of debt that cannot be managed through traditional means. The removal of this enormous burden means that badly needed resources can go to programs that aid needy citizens, just as is intended. However, the HIPC has strict rules that sharply limit this spending. In some cases, teachers are not hired and HIV/AIDS tests are not administered because the sudden spending might lead to macroeconomic instability. This is a paradox that must be confronted: Poor nations need to spend money desperately but wisely.

A more daunting obstacle is the lack of a private sector in many of the countries that are served by the HIPC. Property rights may be virtually non-existent. Without individuals and businesses willing and able to invest resources in their own country, progress can be glacial. Outside investors are forced to deal not with business partners as such, but with governmental agencies ranging from the inept to the murderously corrupt. There is no guarantee that funds meant for a hospital or school will ever find their way to the intended destination, whether because of corruption or the sheer difficulty of moving goods around in a place that is, as is so often the case in truly poor countries, at war.

Debt relief remains an important tool in reducing the terrible suffering that affects so many people in the underdeveloped world. However, it is not enough to clean the slate and say, "start anew." Without the willingness on the part of the governing body to allow its citizens to take part in their own development, and without the right balance of emergency spending and careful investment, unmanageable debt will return, as evidenced by nations that have been borrowing money faster than their debt can be relieved.

45. According to the passage, a nation receiving assistance from the HIPC _____.

    (A) must not be engaged in a war in which it is an aggressor

    (B) must have at least a minimal amount of privately held property, including businesses

    (C) must not have a level of debt that can be managed through a typical debt relief program

    (D) is required to allow ordinary citizens input regarding the use of resources that have been made available through the initiative

    (E) would also be eligible for assistance from the MDRI

Passage 11

Relieving an impoverished country of its debt would seem to almost unavoidably help the citizens of that nation. Indeed, health care and education spending is now greater than debt service payments in many countries that have been granted partial debt relief by the Heavily Indebted Poor Countries (HIPC) Initiative launched by the International Monetary Fund and the World Bank, and complete debt relief by the supplementary Multilateral Debt Relief Initiative (MDRI). Several factors, however, have kept these programs from becoming truly transformational.

For a nation to qualify for the HIPC, it must have a level of debt that cannot be managed through traditional means. The removal of this enormous burden means that badly needed resources can go to programs that aid needy citizens, just as is intended. However, the HIPC has strict rules that sharply limit this spending. In some cases, teachers are not hired and HIV/AIDS tests are not administered because the sudden spending might lead to macroeconomic instability. This is a paradox that must be confronted: Poor nations need to spend money desperately but wisely.

A more daunting obstacle is the lack of a private sector in many of the countries that are served by the HIPC. Property rights may be virtually non-existent. Without individuals and businesses willing and able to invest resources in their own country, progress can be glacial. Outside investors are forced to deal not with business partners as such, but with governmental agencies ranging from the inept to the murderously corrupt. There is no guarantee that funds meant for a hospital or school will ever find their way to the intended destination, whether because of corruption or the sheer difficulty of moving goods around in a place that is, as is so often the case in truly poor countries, at war.

Debt relief remains an important tool in reducing the terrible suffering that affects so many people in the underdeveloped world. However, it is not enough to clean the slate and say, "start anew." Without the willingness on the part of the governing body to allow its citizens to take part in their own development, and without the right balance of emergency spending and careful investment, unmanageable debt will return, as evidenced by nations that have been borrowing money faster than their debt can be relieved.

46. Which of the following can be inferred from the passage regarding some of the nations that have received assistance from the HIPC initiative and from the MDRI?

    (A) They have histories of macroeconomic instability.

    (B) Debt service payments once exceeded the amount of money that was spent on schools and hospitals.

    (C) Property rights had to be established prior to receiving the assistance.

    (D) Civil war sharply limited the amount of debt relief provided.

    (E) The citizens were unwilling to take part in their nations' development.

Passage 12

The ill-fated Home Construction Lending Act of 1901 (the HCLA) was intended to help families pay for the construction of their homes. Americans were flocking to rented apartments in big cities (as were immigrants from around the world), and the biggest supporters of the HCLA were builders and real estate firms located in rural areas. Their hope was that a family that could afford to buy property and build a house in a rural area, as opposed to renting an inexpensive, but crowded and possibly dangerous, apartment in a city, would choose the former. Ostensibly, the HCLA would make it easier for potential homeowners to borrow by providing a federally backed guarantee to the lender, which at the time was more likely to be an insurance company than a bank. In other cases, the government would actually buy the property and pay for the construction of the house. A family could move in and make payments to the government over a much longer period than they could if they were repaying a commercial lender. Unlike the typical amortized 30-year mortgage of today, home loans at the time were usually repaid over three or perhaps five years, and the borrower made a balloon payment of the entire principal at the end of the term. An HCLA loan from the government could be repaid—interest and principal — over as many as 15 years, and did not require a large final payment.

Many lenders, however, did not actually want to have their loans guaranteed, and they resisted providing HCLA loans. For these companies, more profit could be realized by repossessing property when borrowers defaulted on their loans. As to the properties bought and resold by the government, the relatively small payments made at a fixed interest rate cost the government money, and this arrangement was abandoned.

In the same year that saw the passage of the HCLA, the Tenement House Act forced builders in New York to improve the condition of their apartments. Lighting, ventilation, and toilet facilities were improved, and the Tenement House Commission was established to enforce the new law. Other cities followed suit. Urban life was now more attractive to men and women who would have otherwise preferred to live in a rural area, but who needed the employment opportunities that the cities could provide.

47. What is the primary purpose of this passage?

    (A) To describe why the HCLA was passed, and why it proved ineffective

    (B) To provide an overview of the home building situation in the early 20th-century America

    (C) To give an example of a misguided attempt to regulate the urban housing industry

    (D) To contrast the HCLA with current housing and home construction laws

    (E) To elaborate on the reasons that Americans and foreigners flocked to the big cities in the United States during the early 1900s

Passage 12

The ill-fated Home Construction Lending Act of 1901 (the HCLA) was intended to help families pay for the construction of their homes. Americans were flocking to rented apartments in big cities (as were immigrants from around the world), and the biggest supporters of the HCLA were builders and real estate firms located in rural areas. Their hope was that a family that could afford to buy property and build a house in a rural area, as opposed to renting an inexpensive, but crowded and possibly dangerous, apartment in a city, would choose the former. Ostensibly, the HCLA would make it easier for potential homeowners to borrow by providing a federally backed guarantee to the lender, which at the time was more likely to be an insurance company than a bank. In other cases, the government would actually buy the property and pay for the construction of the house. A family could move in and make payments to the government over a much longer period than they could if they were repaying a commercial lender. Unlike the typical amortized 30-year mortgage of today, home loans at the time were usually repaid over three or perhaps five years, and the borrower made a balloon payment of the entire principal at the end of the term. An HCLA loan from the government could be repaid—interest and principal—over as many as 15 years, and did not require a large final payment.

Many lenders, however, did not actually want to have their loans guaranteed, and they resisted providing HCLA loans. For these companies, more profit could be realized by repossessing property when borrowers defaulted on their loans. As to the properties bought and resold by the government, the relatively small payments made at a fixed interest rate cost the government money, and this arrangement was abandoned.

In the same year that saw the passage of the HCLA, the Tenement House Act forced builders in New York to improve the condition of their apartments. Lighting, ventilation, and toilet facilities were improved, and the Tenement House Commission was established to enforce the new law. Other cities followed suit. Urban life was now more attractive to men and women who would have otherwise preferred to live in a rural area, but who needed the employment opportunities that the cities could provide.

48. Which of the following would most appropriately conclude this passage?

   (A) The HCLA could not withstand this migratory push from rural life to city life, and was repealed less than six years after becoming law.

   (B) At the same time, the farming industry was increasingly in the hands of large corporations.

   (C) Even those elected officials who voted against the HCLA were surprised by its unpopularity.

   (D) Though jobs were to be found in the large American cities, adjusting to urban life was still a shock for many young people who arrived at this time.

   (E) The societal effect of the Tenement Housing Act continues to this day.

Passage 12

The ill-fated Home Construction Lending Act of 1901 (the HCLA) was intended to help families pay for the construction of their homes. Americans were flocking to rented apartments in big cities (as were immigrants from around the world), and the biggest supporters of the HCLA were builders and real estate firms located in rural areas. Their hope was that a family that could afford to buy property and build a house in a rural area, as opposed to renting an inexpensive, but crowded and possibly dangerous, apartment in a city, would choose the former. Ostensibly, the HCLA would make it easier for potential homeowners to borrow by providing a federally backed guarantee to the lender, which at the time was more likely to be an insurance company than a bank. In other cases, the government would actually buy the property and pay for the construction of the house. A family could move in and make payments to the government over a much longer period than they could if they were repaying a commercial lender. Unlike the typical amortized 30-year mortgage of today, home loans at the time were usually repaid over three or perhaps five years, and the borrower made a balloon payment of the entire principal at the end of the term. An HCLA loan from the government could be repaid—interest and principal—over as many as 15 years, and did not require a large final payment.

Many lenders, however, did not actually want to have their loans guaranteed, and they resisted providing HCLA loans. For these companies, more profit could be realized by repossessing property when borrowers defaulted on their loans. As to the properties bought and resold by the government, the relatively small payments made at a fixed interest rate cost the government money, and this arrangement was abandoned.

In the same year that saw the passage of the HCLA, the Tenement House Act forced builders in New York to improve the condition of their apartments. Lighting, ventilation, and toilet facilities were improved, and the Tenement House Commission was established to enforce the new law. Other cities followed suit. Urban life was now more attractive to men and women who would have otherwise preferred to live in a rural area, but who needed the employment opportunities that the cities could provide.

49. According to the passage, one reason that the HCLA was expected to increase home construction in rural areas was that, under the HCLA, _____.

    (A) interest rates were lower

    (B) the borrower could make smaller payments

    (C) insurance companies, not banks, loaned the money

    (D) the borrower would not be able to default

    (E) the net cost to the borrower was reduced

Passage 12

The ill-fated Home Construction Lending Act of 1901 (the HCLA) was intended to help families pay for the construction of their homes. Americans were flocking to rented apartments in big cities (as were immigrants from around the world), and the biggest supporters of the HCLA were builders and real estate firms located in rural areas. Their hope was that a family that could afford to buy property and build a house in a rural area, as opposed to renting an inexpensive, but crowded and possibly dangerous, apartment in a city, would choose the former. Ostensibly, the HCLA would make it easier for potential homeowners to borrow by providing a federally backed guarantee to the lender, which at the time was more likely to be an insurance company than a bank. In other cases, the government would actually buy the property and pay for the construction of the house. A family could move in and make payments to the government over a much longer period than they could if they were repaying a commercial lender. Unlike the typical amortized 30-year mortgage of today, home loans at the time were usually repaid over three or perhaps five years, and the borrower made a balloon payment of the entire principal at the end of the term. An HCLA loan from the government could be repaid—interest and principal—over as many as 15 years, and did not require a large final payment.

Many lenders, however, did not actually want to have their loans guaranteed, and they resisted providing HCLA loans. For these companies, more profit could be realized by repossessing property when borrowers defaulted on their loans. As to the properties bought and resold by the government, the relatively small payments made at a fixed interest rate cost the government money, and this arrangement was abandoned.

In the same year that saw the passage of the HCLA, the Tenement House Act forced builders in New York to improve the condition of their apartments. Lighting, ventilation, and toilet facilities were improved, and the Tenement House Commission was established to enforce the new law. Other cities followed suit. Urban life was now more attractive to men and women who would have otherwise preferred to live in a rural area, but who needed the employment opportunities that the cities could provide.

50. According to the passage, the repercussions of the Tenement Housing Act _____.

    (A) provided more employment for people moving to cities from rural areas

    (B) had little effect on builders outside of New York City

    (C) was abandoned because of its cost to the federal government

    (D) convinced some people to try to find work in the big cities of the United States

    (E) led to the passage of the HCLA

Passage 13

Any discussion of how to treat autism is sure to be problematic. To begin with, autism, a neurological condition that impairs an individual's ability to interact with others, is a wide-ranging spectrum disorder. Some high-level autistics hold jobs and have families. Others are almost incapable of communicating or otherwise interacting with the world. Between these extremes lie individuals with a variety of symptoms. Some can communicate, but have difficulty differentiating between a trivial comment and an important point. Others cannot stand to be touched, or might feel a gentle touch as hurtful. As there is no nationwide agreement on the classification of different levels of autism, a person considered to have high-level autism (sometimes called Asperger's Syndrome) could move to a state where he or she is deemed neurotypical—that is, not autistic at all.

Not knowing what causes autism also complicates any consideration of its treatment, though genetic research has proven promising in this regard. A region of chromosome 1 has been associated with autism, as has a region of chromosome 3 that contains the GAT1 gene and the OXTR gene. The GAT1 gene is involved in transmitting messages between brain cells, and the OXTR gene appears to help the early brain develop.

Environmental factors, including viral infections and exposure to environmental chemicals, continue to be investigated as well. There has also been research into the possibility of a link between autism and certain vaccines. None of these possible causes has proven conclusive, but none has been ruled out, either.

Finally, many autistics reject the premise that they need to be "cured" at all. These people, who prefer the term "autistics" to "people with autism," believe that eradicating their autism would wipe out something central to their personalities. Many are opposed to a treatment known as Applied Behavioral Analysis (ABA), arguing that this is a potentially traumatic process that only teaches autistics to imitate certain neurotypical behavior. Some in the autistic community are also critical of neuroleptic drugs, which can suppress certain behaviors, but which, the critics say, are overprescribed. With so much controversy regarding the nature of this complicated condition, it is unlikely that any agreement as to its proper treatment, or whether it should be treated at all, will be forthcoming.

51. The primary purpose of the passage is to _____.

   (A) provide a summary of the range of treatments available for autism

   (B) give a general description of the symptoms and possible causes of autism

   (C) show that autistics are not in agreement as to how to treat their condition, or whether to treat it at all

   (D) reconcile various opinions regarding the treatment of autism

   (E) present an overview of the difficulties involved with treating autism

Passage 13

Any discussion of how to treat autism is sure to be problematic. To begin with, autism, a neurological condition that impairs an individual's ability to interact with others, is a wide-ranging spectrum disorder. Some high-level autistics hold jobs and have families. Others are almost incapable of communicating or otherwise interacting with the world. Between these extremes lie individuals with a variety of symptoms. Some can communicate, but have difficulty differentiating between a trivial comment and an important point. Others cannot stand to be touched, or might feel a gentle touch as hurtful. As there is no nationwide agreement on the classification of different levels of autism, a person considered to have high-level autism (sometimes called Asperger's Syndrome) could move to a state where he or she is deemed neurotypical—that is, not autistic at all.

Not knowing what causes autism also complicates any consideration of its treatment, though genetic research has proven promising in this regard. A region of chromosome 1 has been associated with autism, as has a region of chromosome 3 that contains the GAT1 gene and the OXTR gene. The GAT1 gene is involved in transmitting messages between brain cells, and the OXTR gene appears to help the early brain develop.

Environmental factors, including viral infections and exposure to environmental chemicals, continue to be investigated as well. There has also been research into the possibility of a link between autism and certain vaccines. None of these possible causes has proven conclusive, but none has been ruled out, either.

Finally, many autistics reject the premise that they need to be "cured" at all. These people, who prefer the term "autistics" to "people with autism," believe that eradicating their autism would wipe out something central to their personalities. Many are opposed to a treatment known as Applied Behavioral Analysis (ABA), arguing that this is a potentially traumatic process that only teaches autistics to imitate certain neurotypical behavior. Some in the autistic community are also critical of neuroleptic drugs, which can suppress certain behaviors, but which, the critics say, are overprescribed. With so much controversy regarding the nature of this complicated condition, it is unlikely that any agreement as to its proper treatment, or whether it should be treated at all, will be forthcoming.

52. According to the passage, an autistic individual _____.

    (A) might have developed the condition through exposure to a vaccine

    (B) is symptomatically unlike an individual with Asperger's Syndrome

    (C) given neuroleptic drugs stands a better chance of controlling his or her symptoms than an individual treated with ABA

    (D) who is able to communicate with some proficiency would prefer being called "autistic" not "a person with autism"

    (E) is not able to properly perceive the sense of touch

Passage 13

Any discussion of how to treat autism is sure to be problematic. To begin with, autism, a neurological condition that impairs an individual's ability to interact with others, is a wide-ranging spectrum disorder. Some high-level autistics hold jobs and have families. Others are almost incapable of communicating or otherwise interacting with the world. Between these extremes lie individuals with a variety of symptoms. Some can communicate, but have difficulty differentiating between a trivial comment and an important point. Others cannot stand to be touched, or might feel a gentle touch as hurtful. As there is no nationwide agreement on the classification of different levels of autism, a person considered to have high-level autism (sometimes called Asperger's Syndrome) could move to a state where he or she is deemed neurotypical—that is, not autistic at all.

Not knowing what causes autism also complicates any consideration of its treatment, though genetic research has proven promising in this regard. A region of chromosome 1 has been associated with autism, as has a region of chromosome 3 that contains the GAT1 gene and the OXTR gene. The GAT1 gene is involved in transmitting messages between brain cells, and the OXTR gene appears to help the early brain develop.

Environmental factors, including viral infections and exposure to environmental chemicals, continue to be investigated as well. There has also been research into the possibility of a link between autism and certain vaccines. None of these possible causes has proven conclusive, but none has been ruled out, either.

Finally, many autistics reject the premise that they need to be "cured" at all. These people, who prefer the term "autistics" to "people with autism," believe that eradicating their autism would wipe out something central to their personalities. Many are opposed to a treatment known as Applied Behavioral Analysis (ABA), arguing that this is a potentially traumatic process that only teaches autistics to imitate certain neurotypical behavior. Some in the autistic community are also critical of neuroleptic drugs, which can suppress certain behaviors, but which, the critics say, are overprescribed. With so much controversy regarding the nature of this complicated condition, it is unlikely that any agreement as to its proper treatment, or whether it should be treated at all, will be forthcoming.

53. It can be inferred that individuals who prefer to be called "autistics" rather than "people with autism" _____.

   (A) are likely to have Asperger's Syndrome

   (B) are skeptical that altering someone's GAT1 gene would have any meaningful effect on their autism

   (C) would not be in favor of genetic manipulation as a way to eliminate their autism

   (D) are able to communicate verbally with relative ease

   (E) do not believe that autism is a crucial part of their personalities

Passage 13

Any discussion of how to treat autism is sure to be problematic. To begin with, autism, a neurological condition that impairs an individual's ability to interact with others, is a wide-ranging spectrum disorder. Some high-level autistics hold jobs and have families. Others are almost incapable of communicating or otherwise interacting with the world. Between these extremes lie individuals with a variety of symptoms. Some can communicate, but have difficulty differentiating between a trivial comment and an important point. Others cannot stand to be touched, or might feel a gentle touch as hurtful. As there is no nationwide agreement on the classification of different levels of autism, a person considered to have high-level autism (sometimes called Asperger's Syndrome) could move to a state where he or she is deemed neurotypical—that is, not autistic at all.

Not knowing what causes autism also complicates any consideration of its treatment, though genetic research has proven promising in this regard. A region of chromosome 1 has been associated with autism, as has a region of chromosome 3 that contains the GAT1 gene and the OXTR gene. The GAT1 gene is involved in transmitting messages between brain cells, and the OXTR gene appears to help the early brain develop.

Environmental factors, including viral infections and exposure to environmental chemicals, continue to be investigated as well. There has also been research into the possibility of a link between autism and certain vaccines. None of these possible causes has proven conclusive, but none has been ruled out, either.

Finally, many autistics reject the premise that they need to be "cured" at all. These people, who prefer the term "autistics" to "people with autism," believe that eradicating their autism would wipe out something central to their personalities. Many are opposed to a treatment known as Applied Behavioral Analysis (ABA), arguing that this is a potentially traumatic process that only teaches autistics to imitate certain neurotypical behavior. Some in the autistic community are also critical of neuroleptic drugs, which can suppress certain behaviors, but which, the critics say, are overprescribed. With so much controversy regarding the nature of this complicated condition, it is unlikely that any agreement as to its proper treatment, or whether it should be treated at all, will be forthcoming.

54. According to the passage, brain development in infants _____.

   (A) is largely determined by a region of chromosome 1

   (B) can be affected by environmental chemicals

   (C) is aided by the OXTR gene

   (D) can be damaged by an overprescription of neuroleptic drugs

   (E) can be altered by ABA

Passage 14

The debate over the extent of regulation needed over Internet providers became more heated when, in 2005, the FCC determined that DSL services (technologies that use local telephone networks to transmit digital data) would no longer be controlled by common carrier regulations, but by "net neutrality principles." Net neutrality is a phrase that once applied to technical matters regarding the preference given to data applications over voice and video applications on the Internet, but is now used more broadly to stand for a general evenhandedness when it comes to how network operators (telecommunication firms and cable companies) interact with the content providers who use the networks. Most people take for granted that the network operators have no reason to favor one content provider or Web site over another. If only for practical reasons, however, discrimination of this sort can take place. In order to manage the limited amount of available bandwidth, an operator might slow down a site that uses "too much" bandwidth. Proponents of net neutrality believe that this is unfair, and that limiting bandwidth can be accomplished on the user side, as is done in Australia, without directly punishing the provider.

Interestingly, the battle cry of innovation is heard from both proponents and opponents of net neutrality. Proponents believe that favoring certain applications can slow the adoption of newer, better ones. Even the World Wide Web itself might have been adopted sooner if not for the preference shown for Gopher, a network protocol that preceded the Web. Opponents claim that discrimination of this sort is unavoidable but benign; some packets of information have different latency requirements and must therefore be handled differently. The way to spur innovation, they say, is to minimize government interference, let telecoms and cable companies do what they do best—provide improved products at competitive prices—and let the market separate the winners from the losers.

Currently, the FCC can levy substantial fines for the abuse of the net neutrality principles. It remains to be seen whether the threat of these fines will be enough to ensure that the Internet will be perceived as a level playing field for providers and end users alike.

55. The primary purpose of the passage is to _____.

(A) argue for the expected effectiveness of a change in how the Internet is regulated

(B) discuss some of the issues surrounding a controversial subject

(C) elaborate on the technical matters relating to an issue that affects telecommunication companies

(D) speculate on the future of an industry

(E) summarize the legal arguments surrounding a hotly debated topic

Passage 14

The debate over the extent of regulation needed over Internet providers became more heated when, in 2005, the FCC determined that DSL services (technologies that use local telephone networks to transmit digital data) would no longer be controlled by common carrier regulations, but by "net neutrality principles." Net neutrality is a phrase that once applied to technical matters regarding the preference given to data applications over voice and video applications on the Internet, but is now used more broadly to stand for a general evenhandedness when it comes to how network operators (telecommunication firms and cable companies) interact with the content providers who use the networks. Most people take for granted that the network operators have no reason to favor one content provider or Web site over another. If only for practical reasons, however, discrimination of this sort can take place. In order to manage the limited amount of available bandwidth, an operator might slow down a site that uses "too much" bandwidth. Proponents of net neutrality believe that this is unfair, and that limiting bandwidth can be accomplished on the user side, as is done in Australia, without directly punishing the provider.

Interestingly, the battle cry of innovation is heard from both proponents and opponents of net neutrality. Proponents believe that favoring certain applications can slow the adoption of newer, better ones. Even the World Wide Web itself might have been adopted sooner if not for the preference shown for Gopher, a network protocol that preceded the Web. Opponents claim that discrimination of this sort is unavoidable but benign; some packets of information have different latency requirements and must therefore be handled differently. The way to spur innovation, they say, is to minimize government interference, let telecoms and cable companies do what they do best—provide improved products at competitive prices—and let the market separate the winners from the losers.

Currently, the FCC can levy substantial fines for the abuse of the net neutrality principles. It remains to be seen whether the threat of these fines will be enough to ensure that the Internet will be perceived as a level playing field for providers and end users alike.

56. According to the passage, proponents of net neutrality _____.

    (A) want network providers to give preference to data applications

    (B) were opposed to the FCC ruling that put an end to DSL services being controlled by common carrier regulations

    (C) have been successful in affecting policy in Australia

    (D) believe that it is acceptable to place limits on band width

    (E) are currently in favor of increasing regulatory limits on content providers

Passage 14

The debate over the extent of regulation needed over Internet providers became more heated when, in 2005, the FCC determined that DSL services (technologies that use local telephone networks to transmit digital data) would no longer be controlled by common carrier regulations, but by "net neutrality principles." Net neutrality is a phrase that once applied to technical matters regarding the preference given to data applications over voice and video applications on the Internet, but is now used more broadly to stand for a general evenhandedness when it comes to how network operators (telecommunication firms and cable companies) interact with the content providers who use the networks. Most people take for granted that the network operators have no reason to favor one content provider or Web site over another. If only for practical reasons, however, discrimination of this sort can take place. In order to manage the limited amount of available bandwidth, an operator might slow down a site that uses "too much" bandwidth. Proponents of net neutrality believe that this is unfair, and that limiting bandwidth can be accomplished on the user side, as is done in Australia, without directly punishing the provider.

Interestingly, the battle cry of innovation is heard from both proponents and opponents of net neutrality. Proponents believe that favoring certain applications can slow the adoption of newer, better ones. Even the World Wide Web itself might have been adopted sooner if not for the preference shown for Gopher, a network protocol that preceded the Web. Opponents claim that discrimination of this sort is unavoidable but benign; some packets of information have different latency requirements and must therefore be handled differently. The way to spur innovation, they say, is to minimize government interference, let telecoms and cable companies do what they do best—provide improved products at competitive prices—and let the market separate the winners from the losers.

Currently, the FCC can levy substantial fines for the abuse of the net neutrality principles. It remains to be seen whether the threat of these fines will be enough to ensure that the Internet will be perceived as a level playing field for providers and end users alike.

57. According to the passage, some people believe that latency requirements
_____.

    (A) tend to affect data applications more than video applications

    (B) were not an issue with Gopher

    (C) are an excuse for bandwidth discrimination

    (D) can slow innovation

    (E) are an unnecessary obstacle to making the Internet a level playing
    field

Passage 14

The debate over the extent of regulation needed over Internet providers became more heated when, in 2005, the FCC determined that DSL services (technologies that use local telephone networks to transmit digital data) would no longer be controlled by common carrier regulations, but by "net neutrality principles." Net neutrality is a phrase that once applied to technical matters regarding the preference given to data applications over voice and video applications on the Internet, but is now used more broadly to stand for a general evenhandedness when it comes to how network operators (telecommunication firms and cable companies) interact with the content providers who use the networks. Most people take for granted that the network operators have no reason to favor one content provider or Web site over another. If only for practical reasons, however, discrimination of this sort can take place. In order to manage the limited amount of available bandwidth, an operator might slow down a site that uses "too much" bandwidth. Proponents of net neutrality believe that this is unfair, and that limiting bandwidth can be accomplished on the user side, as is done in Australia, without directly punishing the provider.

Interestingly, the battle cry of innovation is heard from both proponents and opponents of net neutrality. Proponents believe that favoring certain applications can slow the adoption of newer, better ones. Even the World Wide Web itself might have been adopted sooner if not for the preference shown for Gopher, a network protocol that preceded the Web. Opponents claim that discrimination of this sort is unavoidable but benign; some packets of information have different latency requirements and must therefore be handled differently. The way to spur innovation, they say, is to minimize government interference, let telecoms and cable companies do what they do best— provide improved products at competitive prices—and let the market separate the winners from the losers.

Currently, the FCC can levy substantial fines for the abuse of the net neutrality principles. It remains to be seen whether the threat of these fines will be enough to ensure that the Internet will be perceived as a level playing field for providers and end users alike.

58. Which of the following best describes the author's attitude toward the FCC's decision?

   (A) Alarmed, but open-minded

   (B) Distrustful of both sides of the issue

   (C) Optimistic regarding the intent of the decision

   (D) Somewhat enthusiastic

   (E) Generally objective, though cautious

Passage 15

For far too long, the United States has been without a long-range energy plan. The Energy Policy Act of 2005 presents 1,700 pages and several hundred provisions attempting to elucidate such a plan. Many of the Act's provisions are meant to spur innovative technologies, reduce American dependence on foreign oil, and keep a check on prices at the gas pump. These provisions include loan guarantees for companies that develop manufacturing processes that avoid producing greenhouse gases, and tax credits for both manufacturing and using environmentally conscious vehicles and appliances.

Though many of these provisions have merit, the Act is by no means a coherent plan for the future. There is no clear indication as to extent the of the nation's long-term energy needs and no overall mechanism for either meeting those needs or managing the way we do business and live our lives so as to reduce those needs.

What the Act does provide is a slew of tax breaks and incentives for the petroleum, ethanol, and nuclear corporations that are already well served by government largess. And for every environmentally friendly provision, a free pass is given to a major energy provider. Oil and gas industries, for example, have been exempted from some clean-water laws. Another portion of the Act makes it easier to obtain permits for power lines and oil wells on public lands. There is even a provision that would allow for the consolidation of public utilities, something that has been wisely forbidden for the last 80 or so years.

Competition among the big energy concerns might produce innovative and profitable products, but it is folly to leave something so important and complex as the production, distribution, and use of energy to the marketplace alone. The federal government needs to find people who can do the hard science, who understand international markets, and who can formulate a policy that will realistically and conscientiously provide for this country's energy needs as our oil deposits inevitably dry up. A policy of this sort—the Kyoto Protocol—is already in existence, but too many of our politicians are leery of an internationally formulated document that they simplistically see as a giveaway of money and power to developing nations.

59. According to the author, the Energy Policy Act of 2005 _____.

    (A) encourages the consolidation of public utilities

    (B) will do little to affect the price of foreign oil

    (C) will not go far enough in spurring commercial innovation

    (D) did not take into account the interests of smaller energy companies

    (E) contains some useful ideas, but is marred by a lack of comprehensiveness

Passage 15

For far too long, the United States has been without a long-range energy plan. The Energy Policy Act of 2005 presents 1,700 pages and several hundred provisions attempting to elucidate such a plan. Many of the Act's provisions are meant to spur innovative technologies, reduce American dependence on foreign oil, and keep a check on prices at the gas pump. These provisions include loan guarantees for companies that develop manufacturing processes that avoid producing greenhouse gases, and tax credits for both manufacturing and using environmentally conscious vehicles and appliances.

Though many of these provisions have merit, the Act is by no means a coherent plan for the future. There is no clear indication as to extent the of the nation's long-term energy needs and no overall mechanism for either meeting those needs or managing the way we do business and live our lives so as to reduce those needs.

What the Act does provide is a slew of tax breaks and incentives for the petroleum, ethanol, and nuclear corporations that are already well served by government largess. And for every environmentally friendly provision, a free pass is given to a major energy provider. Oil and gas industries, for example, have been exempted from some clean-water laws. Another portion of the Act makes it easier to obtain permits for power lines and oil wells on public lands. There is even a provision that would allow for the consolidation of public utilities, something that has been wisely forbidden for the last 80 or so years.

Competition among the big energy concerns might produce innovative and profitable products, but it is folly to leave something so important and complex as the production, distribution, and use of energy to the marketplace alone. The federal government needs to find people who can do the hard science, who understand international markets, and who can formulate a policy that will realistically and conscientiously provide for this country's energy needs as our oil deposits inevitably dry up. A policy of this sort—the Kyoto Protocol—is already in existence, but too many of our politicians are leery of an internationally formulated document that they simplistically see as a giveaway of money and power to developing nations.

60. The author criticizes the Energy Policy Act of 2005 for all of the following reasons except _____.

   (A) Companies that have already benefited from government policies will receive financial rewards

   (B) There is insufficient mention of how to reduce energy consumption

   (C) The provisions do not properly address the long-terms needs of the American public

   (D) The financial incentives apply only to large businesses

   (E) A longstanding and effective policy is overturned

Passage 15

For far too long, the United States has been without a long-range energy plan. The Energy Policy Act of 2005 presents 1,700 pages and several hundred provisions attempting to elucidate such a plan. Many of the Act's provisions are meant to spur innovative technologies, reduce American dependence on foreign oil, and keep a check on prices at the gas pump. These provisions include loan guarantees for companies that develop manufacturing processes that avoid producing greenhouse gases, and tax credits for both manufacturing and using environmentally conscious vehicles and appliances.

Though many of these provisions have merit, the Act is by no means a coherent plan for the future. There is no clear indication as to extent the of the nation's long-term energy needs and no overall mechanism for either meeting those needs or managing the way we do business and live our lives so as to reduce those needs.

What the Act does provide is a slew of tax breaks and incentives for the petroleum, ethanol, and nuclear corporations that are already well served by government largess. And for every environmentally friendly provision, a free pass is given to a major energy provider. Oil and gas industries, for example, have been exempted from some clean-water laws. Another portion of the Act makes it easier to obtain permits for power lines and oil wells on public lands. There is even a provision that would allow for the consolidation of public utilities, something that has been wisely forbidden for the last 80 or so years.

Competition among the big energy concerns might produce innovative and profitable products, but it is folly to leave something so important and complex as the production, distribution, and use of energy to the marketplace alone. The federal government needs to find people who can do the hard science, who understand international markets, and who can formulate a policy that will realistically and conscientiously provide for this country's energy needs as our oil deposits inevitably dry up. A policy of this sort—the Kyoto Protocol—is already in existence, but too many of our politicians are leery of an internationally formulated document that they simplistically see as a giveaway of money and power to developing nations.

61. According to the author, the Kyoto Protocol _____.

   (A) is marginally better than the Energy Policy Act of 2005

   (B) is viewed with suspicion by some elected officials because of its origins outside of the United States

   (C) will be useful to the United States only after the nation's oil reserves dry up

   (D) was designed by scientists, not politicians

   (E) is more likely to encourage innovation among energy companies than is the Energy Policy Act of 2005

Passage 15

For far too long, the United States has been without a long-range energy plan. The Energy Policy Act of 2005 presents 1,700 pages and several hundred provisions attempting to elucidate such a plan. Many of the Act's provisions are meant to spur innovative technologies, reduce American dependence on foreign oil, and keep a check on prices at the gas pump. These provisions include loan guarantees for companies that develop manufacturing processes that avoid producing greenhouse gases, and tax credits for both manufacturing and using environmentally conscious vehicles and appliances.

Though many of these provisions have merit, the Act is by no means a coherent plan for the future. There is no clear indication as to extent the of the nation's long-term energy needs and no overall mechanism for either meeting those needs or managing the way we do business and live our lives so as to reduce those needs.

What the Act does provide is a slew of tax breaks and incentives for the petroleum, ethanol, and nuclear corporations that are already well served by government largess. And for every environmentally friendly provision, a free pass is given to a major energy provider. Oil and gas industries, for example, have been exempted from some clean-water laws. Another portion of the Act makes it easier to obtain permits for power lines and oil wells on public lands. There is even a provision that would allow for the consolidation of public utilities, something that has been wisely forbidden for the last 80 or so years.

Competition among the big energy concerns might produce innovative and profitable products, but it is folly to leave something so important and complex as the production, distribution, and use of energy to the marketplace alone. The federal government needs to find people who can do the hard science, who understand international markets, and who can formulate a policy that will realistically and conscientiously provide for this country's energy needs as our oil deposits inevitably dry up. A policy of this sort—the Kyoto Protocol—is already in existence, but too many of our politicians are leery of an internationally formulated document that they simplistically see as a giveaway of money and power to developing nations.

62. Which of the following is NOT mentioned in the passage as being a part of the Energy Act of 2005?

   (A) Government aid to ethanol companies

   (B) Guaranteed loans to businesses that avoid producing greenhouse gases as a byproduct of their manufacturing process

   (C) A stricter interpretation of existing clean-water laws

   (D) Expedited access to public lands for private use

   (E) Tax credits for producing appliances that do not harm the environment

Passage 16

It is now commonly accepted that human life originated in East Africa. There is less agreement as to whether the humans that left Africa in a final exodus as recently as 100,000 years ago replaced all other hominids (thus becoming ancestors to everyone now alive) or humans evolved independently in geographically separated regions. Recently, the replacement scenario, as it is sometimes called, has been lent support from genetic research.

Genetic investigations into the origins of human life most often focus on mitochondrial DNA. As opposed to nuclear DNA, mitochondrial DNA is transmitted only from the mother. This allows for the tracing of mutations that arise independently of changes that occur because of the combining of the mother's and father's DNA. As useful as this is, the high mutation rate of mitochondrial DNA allows scientists a look at only relatively recent prehistory. Nuclear DNA, on the other hand, has a low mutation rate, making it ideal for looking into the more distant past. Studying the nuclear DNA of fossils now shows a substantial decrease in population size in Europe and Asia approximately 50—80 thousand years ago. No such decrease happened in Africa. This supports the idea that migrants from Africa replaced all previous humans, and did not interbreed with earlier migrants.

Other research shows less genetic diversity the farther human populations are located from Africa. This difference in diversity, which continues to the present day, also supports the hypothesis that modern human life came from Africa and gradually spread throughout the world. It is worth noting that there is no discontinuity in the decrease of diversity as one travels from Africa; this points to less distinct ethnic and racial divisions than is popularly thought to be the case.

63. Which of the following is the primary purpose of the passage?

    (A) To present statistical evidence that points to a new hypothesis

    (B) To illustrate the ways in which new forms of scientific research can bring about surprising results

    (C) To offer evidence that supports one of two competing theories

    (D) To cast doubt on the reliability of premises that underlie a conclusion

    (E) To describe a model that can be applied to a variety of scientific undertakings

Passage 16

It is now commonly accepted that human life originated in East Africa. There is less agreement as to whether the humans that left Africa in a final exodus as recently as 100,000 years ago replaced all other hominids (thus becoming ancestors to everyone now alive) or humans evolved independently in geographically separated regions. Recently, the replacement scenario, as it is sometimes called, has been lent support from genetic research.

Genetic investigations into the origins of human life most often focus on mitochondrial DNA. As opposed to nuclear DNA, mitochondrial DNA is transmitted only from the mother. This allows for the tracing of mutations that arise independently of changes that occur because of the combining of the mother's and father's DNA. As useful as this is, the high mutation rate of mitochondrial DNA allows scientists a look at only relatively recent prehistory. Nuclear DNA, on the other hand, has a low mutation rate, making it ideal for looking into the more distant past. Studying the nuclear DNA of fossils now shows a substantial decrease in population size in Europe and Asia approximately 50—80 thousand years ago. No such decrease happened in Africa. This supports the idea that migrants from Africa replaced all previous humans, and did not interbreed with earlier migrants.

Other research shows less genetic diversity the farther human populations are located from Africa. This difference in diversity, which continues to the present day, also supports the hypothesis that modern human life came from Africa and gradually spread throughout the world. It is worth noting that there is no discontinuity in the decrease of diversity as one travels from Africa; this points to less distinct ethnic and racial divisions than is popularly thought to be the case.

64. According to the passage, which of the following is NOT characteristic of mitochondrial DNA?

    (A) Transmission comes from the mother only.

    (B) It can be used to trace the origins of human life.

    (C) It is used more frequently than nuclear DNA to study the origin of human life.

    (D) It can be used to investigate distant prehistory.

    (E) It has a relatively high mutation rate.

Passage 16

It is now commonly accepted that human life originated in East Africa. There is less agreement as to whether the humans that left Africa in a final exodus as recently as 100,000 years ago replaced all other hominids (thus becoming ancestors to everyone now alive) or humans evolved independently in geographically separated regions. Recently, the replacement scenario, as it is sometimes called, has been lent support from genetic research.

Genetic investigations into the origins of human life most often focus on mitochondrial DNA. As opposed to nuclear DNA, mitochondrial DNA is transmitted only from the mother. This allows for the tracing of mutations that arise independently of changes that occur because of the combining of the mother's and father's DNA. As useful as this is, the high mutation rate of mitochondrial DNA allows scientists a look at only relatively recent prehistory. Nuclear DNA, on the other hand, has a low mutation rate, making it ideal for looking into the more distant past. Studying the nuclear DNA of fossils now shows a substantial decrease in population size in Europe and Asia approximately 50—80 thousand years ago. No such decrease happened in Africa. This supports the idea that migrants from Africa replaced all previous humans, and did not interbreed with earlier migrants.

Other research shows less genetic diversity the farther human populations are located from Africa. This difference in diversity, which continues to the present day, also supports the hypothesis that modern human life came from Africa and gradually spread throughout the world. It is worth noting that there is no discontinuity in the decrease of diversity as one travels from Africa; this points to less distinct ethnic and racial divisions than is popularly thought to be the case.

65. Which of the following most strongly argues against the replacement scenario?

   (A) Mitochondrial DNA from a human skeleton found in East Africa matches the DNA found in a known route taken by migrants from Africa to Europe.

   (B) Remains have been found of humans in Southeast Asia that developed independently of humans in Central America.

   (C) The DNA from human specimens taken in China and Spain are nearly identical.

   (D) No evidence can be found to support the idea that the first Africans to leave Africa bred with the second group to make the trip.

   (E) DNA from a Neanderthal—an early hominid—shows some similarity with modern human DNA.

Passage 16

It is now commonly accepted that human life originated in East Africa. There is less agreement as to whether the humans that left Africa in a final exodus as recently as 100,000 years ago replaced all other hominids (thus becoming ancestors to everyone now alive) or humans evolved independently in geographically separated regions. Recently, the replacement scenario, as it is sometimes called, has been lent support from genetic research.

Genetic investigations into the origins of human life most often focus on mitochondrial DNA. As opposed to nuclear DNA, mitochondrial DNA is transmitted only from the mother. This allows for the tracing of mutations that arise independently of changes that occur because of the combining of the mother's and father's DNA. As useful as this is, the high mutation rate of mitochondrial DNA allows scientists a look at only relatively recent prehistory. Nuclear DNA, on the other hand, has a low mutation rate, making it ideal for looking into the more distant past. Studying the nuclear DNA of fossils now shows a substantial decrease in population size in Europe and Asia approximately 50—80 thousand years ago. No such decrease happened in Africa. This supports the idea that migrants from Africa replaced all previous humans, and did not interbreed with earlier migrants.

Other research shows less genetic diversity the farther human populations are located from Africa. This difference in diversity, which continues to the present day, also supports the hypothesis that modern human life came from Africa and gradually spread throughout the world. It is worth noting that there is no discontinuity in the decrease of diversity as one travels from Africa; this points to less distinct ethnic and racial divisions than is popularly thought to be the case.

66. According to the passage, which of the following can be inferred about genetic diversity among humans?

    (A) It is easier to detect through the examination of nuclear DNA than through the study of mitochondrial DNA.

    (B) It is affected only by an individual's mother's DNA.

    (C) It has gradually diminished since about 100,000 years ago.

    (D) It is not as ambiguous as most people think.

    (E) The amount of diversity within an existing population can be predicted by its geographic location.

Passage 17

An interesting approach to reducing the Unites States' trade deficit has been suggested: relax export restrictions to China. That this suggestion has come from the President of the People's Republic of China perhaps warrants some skepticism. That this idea is seconded by U.S. trade groups that represent aerospace, software, and microchip manufacturers, all of whom produce equipment that can be used for military purposes, also gives one pause. Despite some reforms, real and promised, China's "private" sector is too entangled with a government whose aims and actions are frequently at odds with U.S. policy and ideology.

To expedite "safe" trade with China, the U.S. has recently compiled a list of acceptable Chinese businesses with which our high-tech firms can trade. This replaces a system that required that exporters take the time—sometimes a considerable amount—to get licenses for the items they wished to export. Supposedly, the new system has stringent criteria that ensure that the Chinese firms will only use the imported goods for non-military purposes. Many of these products are, however, dual-purpose; they have military as well as commercial applications. Despite assurances that ground checks will prevent imported goods from being diverted for military purposes, China is simply too big, and the links between its companies and its government agencies too byzantine, for these assurances to be meaningful.

Another area in which trade with China needs to be handled carefully is that of intellectual property. Here, U.S. companies are largely on their own; our government can establish guidelines and issue warnings, but it cannot take a direct part in legal actions pursued by an American firm that believes its patents, trademarks, or copyrights have been violated. This is no small problem. About 20% of all consumer products in the Chinese market are counterfeit. China's government has taken some steps to address this problem, but these steps have not yet resulted in enough punishment for those who pirate intellectual property to serve as much of a deterrent to others. Furthermore, what the central government promises is one thing; what provincial governments do is another. Corruption, protectionism, and apathy contribute to a climate in which pirating is considered business as usual by local officials located at great distances from the central government.

67. The attitude of the author of the passage toward trade with China is best described as one of _____.

    (A) skeptical advocacy

    (B) disinterested description

    (C) considered wariness

    (D) amused fascination

    (E) troubled confusion

Passage 17

An interesting approach to reducing the Unites States' trade deficit has been suggested: relax export restrictions to China. That this suggestion has come from the President of the People's Republic of China perhaps warrants some skepticism. That this idea is seconded by U.S. trade groups that represent aerospace, software, and microchip manufacturers, all of whom produce equipment that can be used for military purposes, also gives one pause. Despite some reforms, real and promised, China's "private" sector is too entangled with a government whose aims and actions are frequently at odds with U.S. policy and ideology.

To expedite "safe" trade with China, the U.S. has recently compiled a list of acceptable Chinese businesses with which our high-tech firms can trade. This replaces a system that required that exporters take the time—sometimes a considerable amount—to get licenses for the items they wished to export. Supposedly, the new system has stringent criteria that ensure that the Chinese firms will only use the imported goods for non-military purposes. Many of these products are, however, dual-purpose; they have military as well as commercial applications. Despite assurances that ground checks will prevent imported goods from being diverted for military purposes, China is simply too big, and the links between its companies and its government agencies too byzantine, for these assurances to be meaningful.

Another area in which trade with China needs to be handled carefully is that of intellectual property. Here, U.S. companies are largely on their own; our government can establish guidelines and issue warnings, but it cannot take a direct part in legal actions pursued by an American firm that believes its patents, trademarks, or copyrights have been violated. This is no small problem. About 20% of all consumer products in the Chinese market are counterfeit. China's government has taken some steps to address this problem, but these steps have not yet resulted in enough punishment for those who pirate intellectual property to serve as much of a deterrent to others. Furthermore, what the central government promises is one thing; what provincial governments do is another. Corruption, protectionism, and apathy contribute to a climate in which pirating is considered business as usual by local officials located at great distances from the central government.

68. According to the author, the new system of exporting high-tech goods to China _____.

   (A) is an imperfect improvement over the old system

   (B) can take too much time to be truly effective

   (C) will almost certainly be adversely affected by local corruption

   (D) aims to speed up the process of receiving approval for the exportation of some goods

   (E) will only apply to items that can be used for military purposes

Passage 17

An interesting approach to reducing the Unites States' trade deficit has been suggested: relax export restrictions to China. That this suggestion has come from the President of the People's Republic of China perhaps warrants some skepticism. That this idea is seconded by U.S. trade groups that represent aerospace, software, and microchip manufacturers, all of whom produce equipment that can be used for military purposes, also gives one pause. Despite some reforms, real and promised, China's "private" sector is too entangled with a government whose aims and actions are frequently at odds with U.S. policy and ideology.

To expedite "safe" trade with China, the U.S. has recently compiled a list of acceptable Chinese businesses with which our high-tech firms can trade. This replaces a system that required that exporters take the time—sometimes a considerable amount—to get licenses for the items they wished to export. Supposedly, the new system has stringent criteria that ensure that the Chinese firms will only use the imported goods for non-military purposes. Many of these products are, however, dual-purpose; they have military as well as commercial applications. Despite assurances that ground checks will prevent imported goods from being diverted for military purposes, China is simply too big, and the links between its companies and its government agencies too byzantine, for these assurances to be meaningful.

Another area in which trade with China needs to be handled carefully is that of intellectual property. Here, U.S. companies are largely on their own; our government can establish guidelines and issue warnings, but it cannot take a direct part in legal actions pursued by an American firm that believes its patents, trademarks, or copyrights have been violated. This is no small problem. About 20% of all consumer products in the Chinese market are counterfeit. China's government has taken some steps to address this problem, but these steps have not yet resulted in enough punishment for those who pirate intellectual property to serve as much of a deterrent to others. Furthermore, what the central government promises is one thing; what provincial governments do is another. Corruption, protectionism, and apathy contribute to a climate in which pirating is considered business as usual by local officials located at great distances from the central government.

69. One issue that affects both high-tech exports and intellectual property rights is _____.

   (A) the difficulty of knowing what is truly going on in all parts of the country

   (B) that some products intended for commercial use can have military applications

   (C) the lack of interest in monitoring illegal activity of this sort on the part of provincial governments

   (D) the willingness of some American firms to do business with China without due consideration of the political repercussions

   (E) too many of China's products infringe on existing patents, trademarks, and copyrights

Passage 17

An interesting approach to reducing the Unites States' trade deficit has been suggested: relax export restrictions to China. That this suggestion has come from the President of the People's Republic of China perhaps warrants some skepticism. That this idea is seconded by U.S. trade groups that represent aerospace, software, and microchip manufacturers, all of whom produce equipment that can be used for military purposes, also gives one pause. Despite some reforms, real and promised, China's "private" sector is too entangled with a government whose aims and actions are frequently at odds with U.S. policy and ideology.

To expedite "safe" trade with China, the U.S. has recently compiled a list of acceptable Chinese businesses with which our high-tech firms can trade. This replaces a system that required that exporters take the time—sometimes a considerable amount—to get licenses for the items they wished to export. Supposedly, the new system has stringent criteria that ensure that the Chinese firms will only use the imported goods for non-military purposes. Many of these products are, however, dual-purpose; they have military as well as commercial applications. Despite assurances that ground checks will prevent imported goods from being diverted for military purposes, China is simply too big, and the links between its companies and its government agencies too byzantine, for these assurances to be meaningful.

Another area in which trade with China needs to be handled carefully is that of intellectual property. Here, U.S. companies are largely on their own; our government can establish guidelines and issue warnings, but it cannot take a direct part in legal actions pursued by an American firm that believes its patents, trademarks, or copyrights have been violated. This is no small problem. About 20% of all consumer products in the Chinese market are counterfeit. China's government has taken some steps to address this problem, but these steps have not yet resulted in enough punishment for those who pirate intellectual property to serve as much of a deterrent to others. Furthermore, what the central government promises is one thing; what provincial governments do is another. Corruption, protectionism, and apathy contribute to a climate in which pirating is considered business as usual by local officials located at great distances from the central government.

70. Which of the following, if true, would most weaken the author's assumptions regarding the effectiveness of the new system of controlling high-tech trade to China?

    (A) Several local police chiefs in remote provinces have been demoted for taking bribes to not enforce pirating laws.

    (B) New practices in China have led to greater transparency of the connections between companies and government agencies.

    (C) Several U.S. manufacturing firms have expressed reservations regarding the list of acceptable exports.

    (D) The new policy makes clear that any business that exports items that are not on the list of acceptable exports will be subject to large fines, and that the company's chief officers will likely face jail sentences.

    (E) The list of acceptable exports makes clear which ones have military applications.

Passage 18

Recent advances in non-invasive human neuroimaging have provided researchers in the emerging field of social brain science with insights into the workings of consciousness and social cognition. Of special interest is the medial prefrontal cortex (MPFC), a region of the brain associated with memory, fear, and, perhaps, prejudice.

Fears create memories, and those memories appear to be stored in the amygdala. This same region also seems to create memories that counter those fears, though these memories are then stored in the MPFC. Neuroimages show that nerves from the MPFC project into the amygdala, providing the mechanism for suppressing the fear response. As one might expect, rodents with MPFC damage have a decreased ability to deal with certain fears.

MPFC activity also seems to correlate with self-referential judgments and memory. The dorsal MPFC in particular shows heightened activity during introspective mental activity. Interestingly, there is a reduction in ventral MPFC activity when individuals are involved in tasks that demand attention. This indicates that cognitive activity can decrease certain emotional processing. Other differences between these two areas of the MPFC have been noted. The ventral region becomes more engaged when an individual is shown photographs of strangers whose political beliefs—so the viewer is told—are similar to those of the person viewing the photograph, but the dorsal region becomes more active when the photographs are of individuals with whom the viewer does not share the same political perspective.

As long ago as the 19th century, scientists knew that damage to the MPFC interfered with social skills while leaving other mental skills untouched. With our newfound ability to actually observe mental activity in both healthy and impaired individuals without recourse to surgery, we have entered into an area that is sure to provide us with information about ourselves that will prove to be of enormous interest and great usefulness.

71. Which of the following can be inferred from the passage about the ventral MPFC?

    (A) It is in direct contact with the amygdala.

    (B) It is involved in emotional processing.

    (C) It was first identified in the 19th century.

    (D) It is not involved in the storing of memories relating to fears.

    (E) It is smaller than the dorsal MPFC.

Passage 18

Recent advances in non-invasive human neuroimaging have provided researchers in the emerging field of social brain science with insights into the workings of consciousness and social cognition. Of special interest is the medial prefrontal cortex (MPFC), a region of the brain associated with memory, fear, and, perhaps, prejudice.

Fears create memories, and those memories appear to be stored in the amygdala. This same region also seems to create memories that counter those fears, though these memories are then stored in the MPFC. Neuroimages show that nerves from the MPFC project into the amygdala, providing the mechanism for suppressing the fear response. As one might expect, rodents with MPFC damage have a decreased ability to deal with certain fears.

MPFC activity also seems to correlate with self-referential judgments and memory. The dorsal MPFC in particular shows heightened activity during introspective mental activity. Interestingly, there is a reduction in ventral MPFC activity when individuals are involved in tasks that demand attention. This indicates that cognitive activity can decrease certain emotional processing. Other differences between these two areas of the MPFC have been noted. The ventral region becomes more engaged when an individual is shown photographs of strangers whose political beliefs—so the viewer is told—are similar to those of the person viewing the photograph, but the dorsal region becomes more active when the photographs are of individuals with whom the viewer does not share the same political perspective.

As long ago as the 19th century, scientists knew that damage to the MPFC interfered with social skills while leaving other mental skills untouched. With our newfound ability to actually observe mental activity in both healthy and impaired individuals without recourse to surgery, we have entered into an area that is sure to provide us with information about ourselves that will prove to be of enormous interest and great usefulness.

72. The primary purpose of the passage is to _____.

    (A) highlight some of the work being done in a new field

    (B) discuss technological breakthroughs

    (C) illustrate the advantages of non-invasive brain research

    (D) show similarities between apparently differing research methods

    (E) demonstrate the extent to which our knowledge of the brain has increased in recent years

Passage 18

Recent advances in non-invasive human neuroimaging have provided researchers in the emerging field of social brain science with insights into the workings of consciousness and social cognition. Of special interest is the medial prefrontal cortex (MPFC), a region of the brain associated with memory, fear, and, perhaps, prejudice.

Fears create memories, and those memories appear to be stored in the amygdala. This same region also seems to create memories that counter those fears, though these memories are then stored in the MPFC. Neuroimages show that nerves from the MPFC project into the amygdala, providing the mechanism for suppressing the fear response. As one might expect, rodents with MPFC damage have a decreased ability to deal with certain fears.

MPFC activity also seems to correlate with self-referential judgments and memory. The dorsal MPFC in particular shows heightened activity during introspective mental activity. Interestingly, there is a reduction in ventral MPFC activity when individuals are involved in tasks that demand attention. This indicates that cognitive activity can decrease certain emotional processing. Other differences between these two areas of the MPFC have been noted. The ventral region becomes more engaged when an individual is shown photographs of strangers whose political beliefs—so the viewer is told—are similar to those of the person viewing the photograph, but the dorsal region becomes more active when the photographs are of individuals with whom the viewer does not share the same political perspective.

As long ago as the 19th century, scientists knew that damage to the MPFC interfered with social skills while leaving other mental skills untouched. With our newfound ability to actually observe mental activity in both healthy and impaired individuals without recourse to surgery, we have entered into an area that is sure to provide us with information about ourselves that will prove to be of enormous interest and great usefulness.

73. According to the passage, it is likely that the memories that allay fears are

    _____.

    (A) formed in the dorsal and ventral MPFC

    (B) related to memories that form prejudices

    (C) created and stored in different parts of the brain

    (D) able to be manipulated in rats through neuroimaging procedures

    (E) affected by tasks that demand attention

Passage 18

Recent advances in non-invasive human neuroimaging have provided researchers in the emerging field of social brain science with insights into the workings of consciousness and social cognition. Of special interest is the medial prefrontal cortex (MPFC), a region of the brain associated with memory, fear, and, perhaps, prejudice.

Fears create memories, and those memories appear to be stored in the amygdala. This same region also seems to create memories that counter those fears, though these memories are then stored in the MPFC. Neuroimages show that nerves from the MPFC project into the amygdala, providing the mechanism for suppressing the fear response. As one might expect, rodents with MPFC damage have a decreased ability to deal with certain fears.

MPFC activity also seems to correlate with self-referential judgments and memory. The dorsal MPFC in particular shows heightened activity during introspective mental activity. Interestingly, there is a reduction in ventral MPFC activity when individuals are involved in tasks that demand attention. This indicates that cognitive activity can decrease certain emotional processing. Other differences between these two areas of the MPFC have been noted. The ventral region becomes more engaged when an individual is shown photographs of strangers whose political beliefs—so the viewer is told—are similar to those of the person viewing the photograph, but the dorsal region becomes more active when the photographs are of individuals with whom the viewer does not share the same political perspective.

As long ago as the 19th century, scientists knew that damage to the MPFC interfered with social skills while leaving other mental skills untouched. With our newfound ability to actually observe mental activity in both healthy and impaired individuals without recourse to surgery, we have entered into an area that is sure to provide us with information about ourselves that will prove to be of enormous interest and great usefulness.

74. Which of the following does the author NOT mention as being an advantage of neuroimaging?

    (A) Researchers can better understand how people think about themselves.

    (B) The connections between some parts of the brain are made apparent.

    (C) Greater insight as to how people perceive each other is made possible.

    (D) Scientists do not have to rely on animals that have sustained injuries.

    (E) Healthy individuals can be studied through simple surgical procedures.

Passage 19

Twenty years ago, two well-known anthropologists visited Xerox's Research Center to study how people were responding to technological changes and perhaps offer some insights into the company's operations. One of the researchers' suggestions was to put a green start button on the company's copiers. Some people consider this simple advice the beginning of corporate anthropology: the application of analytical skills tradition- ally used to study relatively isolated, tribal societies to understand how corporate employees interact and how consumers consume.

Sid Parkson received his Ph.D. while studying a dwindling society that lived on an Oceanic island with no stores or indoor plumbing. He now works for a software design firm. "Working with various project teams, I am constantly reminded of my fieldwork," says Parkson. "In even the most rigidly hierarchical society, some individuals will wish to change their status, and this can cause friction—not necessarily a bad thing, but I've seen it lead to inferior decision-making, missed deadlines, and soured morale. When the islanders had a problem that threatened a social good, the individuals involved would discuss the issue at a meeting of their leaders—the board of directors, if you will. The higher-ups would say little, but their presence went a long way toward keeping the tone of the debate civilized and focused on the greater good. Follow-up meetings would be held to see whether progress had been made. We've implemented a similar structure here, and it's worked remarkably well, and in the same way."

On the consumer side, corporate anthropology can help to determine whether a product will be used, and how. Rather than using traditional marketing tools such as focus groups and questionnaires, anthropologists closely observe people going about their lives, and determine how a given product might fit into their culture. As with studies that take place within the corporation, physical behavior, language, and social interactions are carefully analyzed and documented.

Some traditional anthropologists are not comfortable with their colleagues serving business interests. Parkson is aware of this and understands these concerns, but he believes that "my job, though it ultimately contributes to a company's bottom line, also contributes to the quality of people's lives. It also provides data on the behavioral patterns of a group of individuals who have something in common, data that are likely to be of interest to others in years to come. That, to me, is the function of anthropology."

75. Which of the following is the author's primary purpose for writing the passage?

   (A) To present a description of corporate anthropology, and to briefly show how it is used and how it is viewed by others

   (B) To define corporate anthropology and show its specific similarities to, and differences with, traditional anthropology

   (C) To demonstrate that anthropology can no longer be viewed as relevant only to isolated tribes

   (D) To offer a detailed analysis of the ways in which corporate anthropology fits within the general description of anthropology

   (E) To make the case that corporate anthropology can be just as useful as traditional anthropology

Passage 19

Twenty years ago, two well-known anthropologists visited Xerox's Research Center to study how people were responding to technological changes and perhaps offer some insights into the company's operations. One of the researchers' suggestions was to put a green start button on the company's copiers. Some people consider this simple advice the beginning of corporate anthropology: the application of analytical skills tradition- ally used to study relatively isolated, tribal societies to understand how corporate employees interact and how consumers consume.

Sid Parkson received his Ph.D. while studying a dwindling society that lived on an Oceanic island with no stores or indoor plumbing. He now works for a software design firm. "Working with various project teams, I am constantly reminded of my fieldwork," says Parkson. "In even the most rigidly hierarchical society, some individuals will wish to change their status, and this can cause friction—not necessarily a bad thing, but I've seen it lead to inferior decision-making, missed deadlines, and soured morale. When the islanders had a problem that threatened a social good, the individuals involved would discuss the issue at a meeting of their leaders—the board of directors, if you will. The higher-ups would say little, but their presence went a long way toward keeping the tone of the debate civilized and focused on the greater good. Follow-up meetings would be held to see whether progress had been made. We've implemented a similar structure here, and it's worked remarkably well, and in the same way."

On the consumer side, corporate anthropology can help to determine whether a product will be used, and how. Rather than using traditional marketing tools such as focus groups and questionnaires, anthropologists closely observe people going about their lives, and determine how a given product might fit into their culture. As with studies that take place within the corporation, physical behavior, language, and social interactions are carefully analyzed and documented.

Some traditional anthropologists are not comfortable with their colleagues serving business interests. Parkson is aware of this and understands these concerns, but he believes that "my job, though it ultimately contributes to a company's bottom line, also contributes to the quality of people's lives. It also provides data on the behavioral patterns of a group of individuals who have something in common, data that are likely to be of interest to others in years to come. That, to me, is the function of anthropology."

76. Which of the following does Sid Parkson claim is common to corporate societies and the lives of the islanders he studied?

   (A) People resent being part of a rigid hierarchical system.

   (B) Morale can be adversely affected by poor decisions.

   (C) Individual members of the societies were sensitive to how their actions affected the common good.

   (D) People behave differently when they know that they are being observed by people of higher status.

   (E) Follow-up meetings to discuss frictions between group members are effective as long as the higher-ups did not take part.

Passage 19

Twenty years ago, two well-known anthropologists visited Xerox's Research Center to study how people were responding to technological changes and perhaps offer some insights into the company's operations. One of the researchers' suggestions was to put a green start button on the company's copiers. Some people consider this simple advice the beginning of corporate anthropology: the application of analytical skills traditionally used to study relatively isolated, tribal societies to understand how corporate employees interact and how consumers consume.

Sid Parkson received his Ph.D. while studying a dwindling society that lived on an Oceanic island with no stores or indoor plumbing. He now works for a software design firm. "Working with various project teams, I am constantly reminded of my fieldwork," says Parkson. "In even the most rigidly hierarchical society, some individuals will wish to change their status, and this can cause friction—not necessarily a bad thing, but I've seen it lead to inferior decision-making, missed deadlines, and soured morale. When the islanders had a problem that threatened a social good, the individuals involved would discuss the issue at a meeting of their leaders—the board of directors, if you will. The higher-ups would say little, but their presence went a long way toward keeping the tone of the debate civilized and focused on the greater good. Follow-up meetings would be held to see whether progress had been made. We've implemented a similar structure here, and it's worked remarkably well, and in the same way."

On the consumer side, corporate anthropology can help to determine whether a product will be used, and how. Rather than using traditional marketing tools such as focus groups and questionnaires, anthropologists closely observe people going about their lives, and determine how a given product might fit into their culture. As with studies that take place within the corporation, physical behavior, language, and social interactions are carefully analyzed and documented.

Some traditional anthropologists are not comfortable with their colleagues serving business interests. Parkson is aware of this and understands these concerns, but he believes that "my job, though it ultimately contributes to a company's bottom line, also contributes to the quality of people's lives. It also provides data on the behavioral patterns of a group of individuals who have something in common, data that are likely to be of interest to others in years to come. That, to me, is the function of anthropology."

77. According to the passage, which of the following scenarios is LEAST likely to be administered by a corporate anthropologist?

    (A) The recordings from a retail store's security camera are analyzed to determine how long people browse before selecting an item.

    (B) A list is compiled that shows the different ways that employees speak about a new product among themselves and to others.

    (C) Teenagers are brought together and their opinions are solicited regarding the desirability of a new portable music player.

    (D) A consultant is hired to observe the manner in which executives at a firm choose to recognize the comments made by employees at business meetings.

    (E) A field trip is arranged so that the managers of a day care center can see how a group of Native Americans handle shared care of children.

Passage 19

Twenty years ago, two well-known anthropologists visited Xerox's Research Center to study how people were responding to technological changes and perhaps offer some insights into the company's operations. One of the researchers' suggestions was to put a green start button on the company's copiers. Some people consider this simple advice the beginning of corporate anthropology: the application of analytical skills traditionally used to study relatively isolated, tribal societies to understand how corporate employees interact and how consumers consume.

Sid Parkson received his Ph.D. while studying a dwindling society that lived on an Oceanic island with no stores or indoor plumbing. He now works for a software design firm. "Working with various project teams, I am constantly reminded of my fieldwork," says Parkson. "In even the most rigidly hierarchical society, some individuals will wish to change their status, and this can cause friction—not necessarily a bad thing, but I've seen it lead to inferior decision-making, missed deadlines, and soured morale. When the islanders had a problem that threatened a social good, the individuals involved would discuss the issue at a meeting of their leaders—the board of directors, if you will. The higher-ups would say little, but their presence went a long way toward keeping the tone of the debate civilized and focused on the greater good. Follow-up meetings would be held to see whether progress had been made. We've implemented a similar structure here, and it's worked remarkably well, and in the same way."

On the consumer side, corporate anthropology can help to determine whether a product will be used, and how. Rather than using traditional marketing tools such as focus groups and questionnaires, anthropologists closely observe people going about their lives, and determine how a given product might fit into their culture. As with studies that take place within the corporation, physical behavior, language, and social interactions are carefully analyzed and documented.

Some traditional anthropologists are not comfortable with their colleagues serving business interests. Parkson is aware of this and understands these concerns, but he believes that "my job, though it ultimately contributes to a company's bottom line, also contributes to the quality of people's lives. It also provides data on the behavioral patterns of a group of individuals who have something in common, data that are likely to be of interest to others in years to come. That, to me, is the function of anthropology."

78. Which of the following is mentioned in the passage as a reason for considering the legitimacy of corporate anthropology?

    (A) There are not enough jobs available for anthropologists who wish to work in academia.

    (B) It can be useful to businesses that wish to improve their profitability.

    (C) It is a way for executives to better understand what motivates their employees.

    (D) Tribal societies can benefit from insights that anthropologists gain from studying corporate cultures.

    (E) It allows people a look at how businesses in the past were structured.

Passage 20

Some of the first attempts to standardize business practices came about during wartime. In World War I, shells frequently failed to detonate simply because two British armament manufacturers had slightly different definitions of an inch. During World War II, Britain placed inspectors in weapons factories to determine the cause of accidental detonations. This led to a system by which potential suppliers had to detail their production processes—and ensure that workers stuck to them—before the supplier could be approved for a government contract. In 1959, the U.S. developed its Quality Program Requirements for military procurement, and NATO followed suit in 1968. By 1987, the UK had formulated the BS9000, one of the first attempts to apply third-party standardization to a non-military manufacturing area: in this case, the electronics industry. Today's ISO9000, a global set of standards used by diverse businesses and governments, can be traced back to the BS9000. The ISO—a non-governmental organization consisting of representatives from 149 countries—has, to date, a portfolio of over 15,000 standards.

Implementation of ISO standards has not always gone smoothly. Too often, a company attempting to conform to standards has created an extra layer of bureaucracy—and all the paperwork that goes along with one—without actually improving processes. In addition, the military origins of the standardization process led to a system that was not always well-suited to businesses that were not traditional factory-floor operations. Recent ISO versions have tried to minimize the emphasis on documentation, and to stress management system effectiveness, process improvement, and customer satisfaction. Like any tool of business, however, ISO standards are used more effectively by some than by others. The difference lies in whether a set of standards is seen as a way to improve business practices or as an annoying checklist of obstacles.

In coming years, more ISO standards will apply to non-manufacturing realms such as the environment, service industries, security, information and communication, and even sociopolitics. Countries that have signed on to the World Trade Organization's Agreement on Technical Barriers to Trade have agreed to ISO assurances that their regulations do not amount to protectionism. International standardization also has the potential to allow developing countries a better chance at competing with businesses from richer nations, though this potential has only begun to be realized.

79. Which of the following is the most appropriate title of the passage?

    (A) How the ISO Became the Standard Bearer of Standards

    (B) Applying Military Methods to the Business World

    (C) The Future of the ISO

    (D) Problems Associated with Implementing Business Standards

    (E) A Brief History of Business Practice Standards

Passage 20

Some of the first attempts to standardize business practices came about during wartime. In World War I, shells frequently failed to detonate simply because two British armament manufacturers had slightly different definitions of an inch. During World War II, Britain placed inspectors in weapons factories to determine the cause of accidental detonations. This led to a system by which potential suppliers had to detail their production processes—and ensure that workers stuck to them—before the supplier could be approved for a government contract. In 1959, the U.S. developed its Quality Program Requirements for military procurement, and NATO followed suit in 1968. By 1987, the UK had formulated the BS9000, one of the first attempts to apply third-party standardization to a non-military manufacturing area: in this case, the electronics industry. Today's ISO9000, a global set of standards used by diverse businesses and governments, can be traced back to the BS9000. The ISO—a non-governmental organization consisting of representatives from 149 countries—has, to date, a portfolio of over 15,000 standards.

Implementation of ISO standards has not always gone smoothly. Too often, a company attempting to conform to standards has created an extra layer of bureaucracy—and all the paperwork that goes along with one—without actually improving processes. In addition, the military origins of the standardization process led to a system that was not always well-suited to businesses that were not traditional factory-floor operations. Recent ISO versions have tried to minimize the emphasis on documentation, and to stress management system effectiveness, process improvement, and customer satisfaction. Like any tool of business, however, ISO standards are used more effectively by some than by others. The difference lies in whether a set of standards is seen as a way to improve business practices or as an annoying checklist of obstacles.

In coming years, more ISO standards will apply to non-manufacturing realms such as the environment, service industries, security, information and communication, and even sociopolitics. Countries that have signed on to the World Trade Organization's Agreement on Technical Barriers to Trade have agreed to ISO assurances that their regulations do not amount to protectionism. International standardization also has the potential to allow developing countries a better chance at competing with businesses from richer nations, though this potential has only begun to be realized.

80. According to the passage, which of the following has been true of third-party standardization of the British electronics industry?

    (A) It has invariably led businesses to create extra layers of bureaucracy.

    (B) It has led to the formulation of the ISO9000.

    (C) It was created while Britain was at war.

    (D) Some of the standard practices were used by the military.

    (E) It was based on the Quality Program Requirements devised by the U.S..

Passage 20

Some of the first attempts to standardize business practices came about during wartime. In World War I, shells frequently failed to detonate simply because two British armament manufacturers had slightly different definitions of an inch. During World War II, Britain placed inspectors in weapons factories to determine the cause of accidental detonations. This led to a system by which potential suppliers had to detail their production processes—and ensure that workers stuck to them—before the supplier could be approved for a government contract. In 1959, the U.S. developed its Quality Program Requirements for military procurement, and NATO followed suit in 1968. By 1987, the UK had formulated the BS9000, one of the first attempts to apply third-party standardization to a non-military manufacturing area: in this case, the electronics industry. Today's ISO9000, a global set of standards used by diverse businesses and governments, can be traced back to the BS9000. The ISO—a non-governmental organization consisting of representatives from 149 countries—has, to date, a portfolio of over 15,000 standards.

Implementation of ISO standards has not always gone smoothly. Too often, a company attempting to conform to standards has created an extra layer of bureaucracy—and all the paperwork that goes along with one—without actually improving processes. In addition, the military origins of the standardization process led to a system that was not always well-suited to businesses that were not traditional factory-floor operations. Recent ISO versions have tried to minimize the emphasis on documentation, and to stress management system effectiveness, process improvement, and customer satisfaction. Like any tool of business, however, ISO standards are used more effectively by some than by others. The difference lies in whether a set of standards is seen as a way to improve business practices or as an annoying checklist of obstacles.

In coming years, more ISO standards will apply to non-manufacturing realms such as the environment, service industries, security, information and communication, and even sociopolitics. Countries that have signed on to the World Trade Organization's Agreement on Technical Barriers to Trade have agreed to ISO assurances that their regulations do not amount to protectionism. International standardization also has the potential to allow developing countries a better chance at competing with businesses from richer nations, though this potential has only begun to be realized.

81. The passage suggests that implementing ISO standards has led some businesses to _____.

    (A) make changes that have not been productive

    (B) create environmentally harmless manufacturing processes

    (C) adopt some of the same managerial practices of military operations

    (D) identify new methods with which to gauge customer satisfaction

    (E) improve their own internal standards

Passage 20

Some of the first attempts to standardize business practices came about during wartime. In World War I, shells frequently failed to detonate simply because two British armament manufacturers had slightly different definitions of an inch. During World War II, Britain placed inspectors in weapons factories to determine the cause of accidental detonations. This led to a system by which potential suppliers had to detail their production processes—and ensure that workers stuck to them—before the supplier could be approved for a government contract. In 1959, the U.S. developed its Quality Program Requirements for military procurement, and NATO followed suit in 1968. By 1987, the UK had formulated the BS9000, one of the first attempts to apply third-party standardization to a non-military manufacturing area: in this case, the electronics industry. Today's ISO9000, a global set of standards used by diverse businesses and governments, can be traced back to the BS9000. The ISO—a non-governmental organization consisting of representatives from 149 countries—has, to date, a portfolio of over 15,000 standards.

Implementation of ISO standards has not always gone smoothly. Too often, a company attempting to conform to standards has created an extra layer of bureaucracy—and all the paperwork that goes along with one—without actually improving processes. In addition, the military origins of the standardization process led to a system that was not always well-suited to businesses that were not traditional factory-floor operations. Recent ISO versions have tried to minimize the emphasis on documentation, and to stress management system effectiveness, process improvement, and customer satisfaction. Like any tool of business, however, ISO standards are used more effectively by some than by others. The difference lies in whether a set of standards is seen as a way to improve business practices or as an annoying checklist of obstacles.

In coming years, more ISO standards will apply to non-manufacturing realms such as the environment, service industries, security, information and communication, and even sociopolitics. Countries that have signed on to the World Trade Organization's Agreement on Technical Barriers to Trade have agreed to ISO assurances that their regulations do not amount to protectionism. International standardization also has the potential to allow developing countries a better chance at competing with businesses from richer nations, though this potential has only begun to be realized.

82. The passage suggests which of the following about the future of international standardization?

    (A) Developing nations will take a greater part in devising the standards.

    (B) ISO standards will be less useful to traditional factory-floor operations.

    (C) Security concerns will be addressed by a greater number of ISO standards.

    (D) A greater number of businesses will use the standards to improve their practices.

    (E) It will be used to punish countries that practice protectionism.

Passage 21

One clear advantage of selling goods online is that smaller markets can be served without the seller needing to invest in heavy inventory costs. Recordings of classical music, for example, are increasingly hard to find at the larger music chains, where only a handful of recordings sell well enough to make the inventory costs and use of shelf space worthwhile, but the aficionado can now locate nearly any classical CD in print on the Internet. In addition, forward-thinking artists without national reputations have made their music available on personal sites or through services that provide the musicians a more generous share of profits than that offered by the large record labels. For some, this has resulted in increased sales volume, greater return on investment, greater control of product, and a more direct connection with an eager market base. Major orchestras and record labels have taken note, and have created Web sites where one can purchase individual tracks, full CDs, archival recordings, and even music exclusively made available for online downloads. Some symphony orchestras now include, with the price of admission to a concert, the right to download a recording of the concert afterward. Other services allow the listener unlimited streaming or downloading for a monthly fee.

The question remains as to whether classical music will remain at the periphery of the online market, just as it is in the big retail chains. The short answer is most likely yes; classical music is now just one more niche market, albeit one with a particularly long and distinguished past. Cultural factors—most notably television—have been at work for some time now, creating a limited audience for music that requires sustained critical listening. However, the digital economy has ensured two important factors. First, for those with an interest, an impressively wide range of classical music will be available for some time to come. Second, motivated new artists can earn enough to continue to produce new recordings.

83. The primary purpose of the passage is to _____.

   (A) demonstrate that classical music, though it is part of a culture that is antithetical to its existence, will exist for some time to come

   (B) acknowledge that classical music sales are unlikely to capture a significantly larger part of the market share of musical recordings, despite the beneficial effect of online sales

   (C) discuss the many ways that the Internet has contributed, and will contribute, to sales of smaller markets

   (D) use the effect that online sales has had – and will have – on classical music sales as an example of how the digital economy can change smaller markets

   (E) show how a few motivated artists have revolutionized a field that was in danger of becoming extinct

Passage 21

One clear advantage of selling goods online is that smaller markets can be served without the seller needing to invest in heavy inventory costs. Recordings of classical music, for example, are increasingly hard to find at the larger music chains, where only a handful of recordings sell well enough to make the inventory costs and use of shelf space worthwhile, but the aficionado can now locate nearly any classical CD in print on the Internet. In addition, forward-thinking artists without national reputations have made their music available on personal sites or through services that provide the musicians a more generous share of profits than that offered by the large record labels. For some, this has resulted in increased sales volume, greater return on investment, greater control of product, and a more direct connection with an eager market base. Major orchestras and record labels have taken note, and have created Web sites where one can purchase individual tracks, full CDs, archival recordings, and even music exclusively made available for online downloads. Some symphony orchestras now include, with the price of admission to a concert, the right to download a recording of the concert afterward. Other services allow the listener unlimited streaming or downloading for a monthly fee.

The question remains as to whether classical music will remain at the periphery of the online market, just as it is in the big retail chains. The short answer is most likely yes; classical music is now just one more niche market, albeit one with a particularly long and distinguished past. Cultural factors—most notably television—have been at work for some time now, creating a limited audience for music that requires sustained critical listening. However, the digital economy has ensured two important factors. First, for those with an interest, an impressively wide range of classical music will be available for some time to come. Second, motivated new artists can earn enough to continue to produce new recordings.

84. It can be inferred from the passage that the author believes that _____.

   (A) classical music recordings available exclusively online are equal to those available in stores

   (B) the large music chains have not done enough to promote the sales of classical music recordings

   (C) the enjoyment of popular music does not necessitate long periods of intense listening

   (D) any classical musician who wishes to increase sales of his or her recordings should set up a personal Web site

   (E) the digital economy has had a mixed effect on classical music sales

Passage 21

One clear advantage of selling goods online is that smaller markets can be served without the seller needing to invest in heavy inventory costs. Recordings of classical music, for example, are increasingly hard to find at the larger music chains, where only a handful of recordings sell well enough to make the inventory costs and use of shelf space worthwhile, but the aficionado can now locate nearly any classical CD in print on the Internet. In addition, forward-thinking artists without national reputations have made their music available on personal sites or through services that provide the musicians a more generous share of profits than that offered by the large record labels. For some, this has resulted in increased sales volume, greater return on investment, greater control of product, and a more direct connection with an eager market base. Major orchestras and record labels have taken note, and have created Web sites where one can purchase individual tracks, full CDs, archival recordings, and even music exclusively made available for online downloads. Some symphony orchestras now include, with the price of admission to a concert, the right to download a recording of the concert afterward. Other services allow the listener unlimited streaming or downloading for a monthly fee.

The question remains as to whether classical music will remain at the periphery of the online market, just as it is in the big retail chains. The short answer is most likely yes; classical music is now just one more niche market, albeit one with a particularly long and distinguished past. Cultural factors—most notably television—have been at work for some time now, creating a limited audience for music that requires sustained critical listening. However, the digital economy has ensured two important factors. First, for those with an interest, an impressively wide range of classical music will be available for some time to come. Second, motivated new artists can earn enough to continue to produce new recordings.

85. Which of the following is NOT an example of the effect that the digital economy has had on the selling of classical music, as described in the passage?

    (A) Consumers are able to purchase CDs that are unavailable in stores.

    (B) Artists find it easier to send promotional information to people who have expressed an interest in the artists' music.

    (C) A major record label offers its new artists a greater share of profits than in the past.

    (D) Listeners download music without having to concern themselves with the cost of each download.

    (E) A new artist sells enough copies of a first CD to pay for the production of a second.

Passage 21

One clear advantage of selling goods online is that smaller markets can be served without the seller needing to invest in heavy inventory costs. Recordings of classical music, for example, are increasingly hard to find at the larger music chains, where only a handful of recordings sell well enough to make the inventory costs and use of shelf space worthwhile, but the aficionado can now locate nearly any classical CD in print on the Internet. In addition, forward-thinking artists without national reputations have made their music available on personal sites or through services that provide the musicians a more generous share of profits than that offered by the large record labels. For some, this has resulted in increased sales volume, greater return on investment, greater control of product, and a more direct connection with an eager market base. Major orchestras and record labels have taken note, and have created Web sites where one can purchase individual tracks, full CDs, archival recordings, and even music exclusively made available for online downloads. Some symphony orchestras now include, with the price of admission to a concert, the right to download a recording of the concert afterward. Other services allow the listener unlimited streaming or downloading for a monthly fee.

The question remains as to whether classical music will remain at the periphery of the online market, just as it is in the big retail chains. The short answer is most likely yes; classical music is now just one more niche market, albeit one with a particularly long and distinguished past. Cultural factors—most notably television—have been at work for some time now, creating a limited audience for music that requires sustained critical listening. However, the digital economy has ensured two important factors. First, for those with an interest, an impressively wide range of classical music will be available for some time to come. Second, motivated new artists can earn enough to continue to produce new recordings.

86. It can be inferred from the passage that one factor that has led to the marginalizing of classical music in retail stores is that _____.

   (A) classical music must compete with a wide range of other niche market recordings

   (B) physical space is needed for better-selling recordings

   (C) major orchestras have had a difficult time selling tickets to live performances

   (D) inventory costs of classical music recordings tend to be higher than those associated with popular music

   (E) recordings are displayed in a way that is disadvantageous to the consumer who is interested in a recording that is not a big seller

Passage 22

Franklin Delano Roosevelt's New Deal was hotly debated at the time it was instituted, and amazingly, it is still a sensitive topic for ideologues on the left and right today. Whether Roosevelt's overhauling of the economy brought the U.S. out of the Great Depression or prolonged it, as some believe, there is little disagreement as to the magnifying effect that his policies had on the ability and propensity of the federal government to involve itself in the nation's economic affairs, by legislative means or by direct expenditures. New Deal emergency relief programs gave the government control over labor laws, transportation regulations, and farming methods, not to mention criminal law and even social welfare. Prior to the New Deal, banks were regulated by the states, though the Federal Reserve Bank, sometimes referred to as a decentralized central bank, was in place by 1913.

Any wartime effort is sure to increase federal power, and World War II solidified the expectation that the executive branch in particular could, for better or worse, have a large hand in controlling economic and business policy. The bond between the military and the industrial sector, which had been so important in winning the war, gave rise to what President Eisenhower called, with some foreboding, the military-industrial complex. When John Kennedy took office during economically promising times, he announced his New Frontier program, now often remembered for its boosterism of the space program, but which also gave the government added powers to negotiate tariff reductions and take part in multinational trade negotiations. Amendments to the Fair Labor Standards Act increased both the minimum wage and the number of workers in the retail sector that were to be covered. An ambitious housing bill increased the government's involvement in authorizing mortgages for home rehabilitation and providing grants for urban renewal.

Though the expansion of federal economic activism has been associated with Democrats since the time of Roosevelt, Republican Richard Nixon did not shy from federal involvement in non-emergency economic issues. It wasn't until the presidency of Ronald Reagan that an attempt was made to scale back government influence in economic and business affairs so that the famous—and debatable— "invisible hand" of capitalism could guide the economy and promote social good.

87. Which of the following is the most appropriate title of the passage?

    (A) How the New Deal Increased Federal Spending

    (B) The Economic and Social Impact of Executive Branch Spending

    (C) The New Deal's Legacy of Federal Economic Activism

    (D) Government Control of Monetary Policy Since the New Deal

    (E) The Path from Government Activism to the Invisible Hand

Passage 22

Franklin Delano Roosevelt's New Deal was hotly debated at the time it was instituted, and amazingly, it is still a sensitive topic for ideologues on the left and right today. Whether Roosevelt's overhauling of the economy brought the U.S. out of the Great Depression or prolonged it, as some believe, there is little disagreement as to the magnifying effect that his policies had on the ability and propensity of the federal government to involve itself in the nation's economic affairs, by legislative means or by direct expenditures. New Deal emergency relief programs gave the government control over labor laws, transportation regulations, and farming methods, not to mention criminal law and even social welfare. Prior to the New Deal, banks were regulated by the states, though the Federal Reserve Bank, sometimes referred to as a decentralized central bank, was in place by 1913.

Any wartime effort is sure to increase federal power, and World War II solidified the expectation that the executive branch in particular could, for better or worse, have a large hand in controlling economic and business policy. The bond between the military and the industrial sector, which had been so important in winning the war, gave rise to what President Eisenhower called, with some foreboding, the military-industrial complex. When John Kennedy took office during economically promising times, he announced his New Frontier program, now often remembered for its boosterism of the space program, but which also gave the government added powers to negotiate tariff reductions and take part in multinational trade negotiations. Amendments to the Fair Labor Standards Act increased both the minimum wage and the number of workers in the retail sector that were to be covered. An ambitious housing bill increased the government's involvement in authorizing mortgages for home rehabilitation and providing grants for urban renewal.

Though the expansion of federal economic activism has been associated with Democrats since the time of Roosevelt, Republican Richard Nixon did not shy from federal involvement in non-emergency economic issues. It wasn't until the presidency of Ronald Reagan that an attempt was made to scale back government influence in economic and business affairs so that the famous—and debatable—"invisible hand" of capitalism could guide the economy and promote social good.

88. It can be inferred from the passage that the New Deal _____.

   (A) turned regulation of the banks over to the federal government

   (B) created the Federal Reserve Bank as a means of gaining more control over economic policy

   (C) was responsible for the federal government's first attempt at directly promoting social welfare programs

   (D) came to an end with the start of World War II

   (E) was unpopular with labor leaders whose actions were increasingly overseen by the executive branch of the government

Passage 22

Franklin Delano Roosevelt's New Deal was hotly debated at the time it was instituted, and amazingly, it is still a sensitive topic for ideologues on the left and right today. Whether Roosevelt's overhauling of the economy brought the U.S. out of the Great Depression or prolonged it, as some believe, there is little disagreement as to the magnifying effect that his policies had on the ability and propensity of the federal government to involve itself in the nation's economic affairs, by legislative means or by direct expenditures. New Deal emergency relief programs gave the government control over labor laws, transportation regulations, and farming methods, not to mention criminal law and even social welfare. Prior to the New Deal, banks were regulated by the states, though the Federal Reserve Bank, sometimes referred to as a decentralized central bank, was in place by 1913.

Any wartime effort is sure to increase federal power, and World War II solidified the expectation that the executive branch in particular could, for better or worse, have a large hand in controlling economic and business policy. The bond between the military and the industrial sector, which had been so important in winning the war, gave rise to what President Eisenhower called, with some foreboding, the military-industrial complex. When John Kennedy took office during economically promising times, he announced his New Frontier program, now often remembered for its boosterism of the space program, but which also gave the government added powers to negotiate tariff reductions and take part in multinational trade negotiations. Amendments to the Fair Labor Standards Act increased both the minimum wage and the number of workers in the retail sector that were to be covered. An ambitious housing bill increased the government's involvement in authorizing mortgages for home rehabilitation and providing grants for urban renewal.

Though the expansion of federal economic activism has been associated with Democrats since the time of Roosevelt, Republican Richard Nixon did not shy from federal involvement in non-emergency economic issues. It wasn't until the presidency of Ronald Reagan that an attempt was made to scale back government influence in economic and business affairs so that the famous—and debatable—"invisible hand" of capitalism could guide the economy and promote social good.

89. According to the passage, which of the following was NOT necessarily true of the New Frontier?

(A) It addressed the need for loans with which to improve housing.

(B) It gave the federal government a larger role to play in some global affairs.

(C) It was enacted during a time when the future of the economy looked bright.

(D) It was instrumental in creating the Fair Labor Standards Act.

(E) It guaranteed wages for a greater number of people.

Passage 22

Franklin Delano Roosevelt's New Deal was hotly debated at the time it was instituted, and amazingly, it is still a sensitive topic for ideologues on the left and right today. Whether Roosevelt's overhauling of the economy brought the U.S. out of the Great Depression or prolonged it, as some believe, there is little disagreement as to the magnifying effect that his policies had on the ability and propensity of the federal government to involve itself in the nation's economic affairs, by legislative means or by direct expenditures. New Deal emergency relief programs gave the government control over labor laws, transportation regulations, and farming methods, not to mention criminal law and even social welfare. Prior to the New Deal, banks were regulated by the states, though the Federal Reserve Bank, sometimes referred to as a decentralized central bank, was in place by 1913.

Any wartime effort is sure to increase federal power, and World War II solidified the expectation that the executive branch in particular could, for better or worse, have a large hand in controlling economic and business policy. The bond between the military and the industrial sector, which had been so important in winning the war, gave rise to what President Eisenhower called, with some foreboding, the military-industrial complex. When John Kennedy took office during economically promising times, he announced his New Frontier program, now often remembered for its boosterism of the space program, but which also gave the government added powers to negotiate tariff reductions and take part in multinational trade negotiations. Amendments to the Fair Labor Standards Act increased both the minimum wage and the number of workers in the retail sector that were to be covered. An ambitious housing bill increased the government's involvement in authorizing mortgages for home rehabilitation and providing grants for urban renewal.

Though the expansion of federal economic activism has been associated with Democrats since the time of Roosevelt, Republican Richard Nixon did not shy from federal involvement in non-emergency economic issues. It wasn't until the presidency of Ronald Reagan that an attempt was made to scale back government influence in economic and business affairs so that the famous—and debatable—"invisible hand" of capitalism could guide the economy and promote social good.

90. It can be inferred from the passage that federal involvement in business affairs
_____.

   (A) became associated with Republicans after Richard Nixon took office

   (B) was discouraged by those who believed that the "invisible hand" of capitalism would produce non-economic benefits

   (C) was responsible for the creation of a so-called "military-industrial" complex

   (D) was never the intent of the New Frontier, though it was essential to the implementation of the New Deal

   (E) is most effective when it is reserved for economic emergencies such as those created by the Great Depression

ANSWER KEY

LESSONS

1.	E	17.	C
2.	D		
3.	E		
4.	C		
5.	D		
6.	A		
7.	C		
8.	C		
9.	D		
10.	B		
11.	E		
12.	C		
13.	D		
14.	C		
15.	B		
16.	C		

HOMEWORK

18.	C	34.	D	50.	D	66.	E	82.	C
19.	A	35.	E	51.	E	67.	C	83.	D
20.	E	36.	B	52.	A	68.	D	84.	C
21.	D	37.	C	53.	C	69.	A	85.	C
22.	D	38.	B	54.	C	70.	B	86.	B
23.	A	39.	D	55.	B	71.	B	87.	C
24.	C	40.	A	56.	D	72.	A	88.	A
25.	C	41.	B	57.	C	73.	C	89.	D
26.	E	42.	E	58.	E	74.	E	90.	B
27.	A	43.	B	59.	E	75.	A		
28.	C	44.	D	60.	D	76.	D		
29.	D	45.	C	61.	B	77.	C		
30.	C	46.	B	62.	C	78.	E		
31.	D	47.	A	63.	C	79.	E		
32.	B	48.	A	64.	D	80.	B		
33.	C	49.	B	65.	B	81.	A